ABSOLUTE BEGINNER'S GUIDE

Keynote™ for Mac OS® X

Curt Simmons

800 East 96th Street,
Indianapolis, Indiana 46240

Absolute Beginner's Guide to Keynote™ for Mac OS® X

International Standard Book Number: 0-7897-3101-0

Library of Congress Catalog Card Number: 2003114785

Printed in the United States of America

First Printing: March 2004

07 06 05 04   4 3 2 1

Trademarks

All terms mentioned in this book that are known to be trademarks or service marks have been appropriately capitalized. Que Publishing cannot attest to the accuracy of this information. Use of a term in this book should not be regarded as affecting the validity of any trademark or service mark.

Keynote is a trademark of Apple Computer, Inc.

Mac OS is a registered trademark of Apple Computer, Inc.

Warning and Disclaimer

Every effort has been made to make this book as complete and as accurate as possible, but no warranty or fitness is implied. The information provided is on an "as is" basis. The author and the publisher shall have neither liability nor responsibility to any person or entity with respect to any loss or damages arising from the information contained in this book.

Bulk Sales

Que offers excellent discounts on this book when ordered in quantity for bulk purchases or special sales. For more information, please contact:

U.S. Corporate and Government Sales
1-800-382-3419
corpsales@pearsontechgroup.com

For sales outside of the U.S., please contact:

International Sales
1-317-428-3341
international@pearsontechgroup.com

Associate Publisher
Greg Wiegand

Executive Editor
Rick Kughen

Development Editor
Laura Norman

Managing Editor
Charlotte Clapp

Project Editor
Tonya Simpson

Copy Editor
Kitty Jarrett

Indexer
Erika Millen

Proofreader
Kathy Bidwell

Technical Editor
Brian Hubbard

Team Coordinator
Sharry Lee Gregory

Interior Designer
Anne Jones

Cover Designer
Dan Armstrong

Page Layout
Stacey Richwine-DeRome

Contents at a Glance

	Introduction	.1
1	Beginning Skills: Getting to Know Keynote	.5
2	Working with Text	.27
3	Using Tables	.47
4	Using Charts	.65
5	Working with Graphics	.89
6	Working with Backgrounds and Multimedia	.117
7	Managing Your Presentation	.135
8	Exploring Transitions and Builds	.155
9	Showing Your Stuff: Making Your Presentation	.173
10	Extending Keynote	.187
A	Installing Keynote	.199
B	Keyboard Shortcuts	.203
C	Helpful Keynote Web Sites	.209
	Index	.211

Table of Contents

Introduction 1

Public Speaking—Then and Now 1

Enter the World of Keynote 2

How to Use This Book 2

Conventions Used in This Book 3
 Web Page Addresses 4
 Special Elements 4

1 Beginning Skills: Getting to Know Keynote 5

What Keynote Is All About 6

What Keynote Can Do 7

Working with the Keynote Screen 8

Introducing the Inspector 9

Creating Your First Presentation 10
 Understanding Themes 11
 Introducing Master Slides 12
 Adding Text to a Slide 12
 Adding Slides 13

Creating Tables in Slides 14
 Incorporating Charts in Slides 15
 Including Graphic Images in Slides 17

Organizing Slides 20
 Choosing a View 20
 Rearranging and Grouping Slides 21

Playing the Slideshow 22

Saving Your Work 23

Introducing Builds 23

Introducing Transitions 25

2 Working with Text **27**

The Truth About Presentation Text **28**
Make the Text Easy to Read 28
Highlight Main Ideas 31
Watch Your Spelling and Punctuation 32
Don't Overcrowd 33

Entering Text on Slides **33**
Deleting a Text Box 34
Adding a Text Box 35

Working with Fonts and Styles **36**

Using the Text Inspector **39**
Changing Text Color 39
Managing Text Alignment and Spacing 40

Using Bullets and Numbering **42**

Setting Text Tabs **45**

Importing Text **45**

3 Using Tables **47**

The Wonderful World of Tables **48**

Creating a Table **49**

Moving Around in a Table **50**

Entering and Formatting Text **51**
Aligning Text 53
Quick Text Tricks 55

Formatting Cells, Rows, and Columns **56**
Choosing the Number of Columns and Rows in a Table 56
Merging and Splitting Rows and Columns 57
Adjusting the Cell Border 59
Choosing the Cell Background 61

Inserting Graphics in Tables **62**

4 Using Charts **65**

The Wonderful World of Charts **66**

Creating a Chart **67**

Choosing a Chart Style **69**
Column Charts 70
Stacked Column Charts 70
Bar Charts 70
Stacked Bar Charts 71
Line Charts 71
Area Charts 72
Stacked Area Charts 73
Pie Charts 73

Working with Chart Data **73**
Understanding Chart Data 74
Using the Chart Data Editor 74
Using the Chart Inspector 77

Formatting Charts **79**
Moving the Chart Legend 79
Changing Chart Colors 80
Changing Chart Fonts 81
Working with Labels and Axis Markings 82
Formatting Data Series Elements 84

Special Issues with Pie Charts **86**

5 Working with Graphics **89**

Understanding How to Use Graphics in Presentations **90**
Using Graphics to Make Text Easier to Understand 90
Using Graphic Shapes to Enhance Presentations 91
Using Photos in Presentations 92

Working with the Colors Dialog Box **92**
Color Wheel 93
Color Sliders 93
Color Palettes 94
Image Palettes 95
Crayons 95

Working with Line Art **96**
   Inserting Shapes 96
   Filling a Shape with Color 97
   Stroke 101
   Shadow 101

Working with Images **103**
   Importing Photos 103
   Using Keynote's Image Library 105

Using Alignment Guides to Precisely Position Text and Objects **106**
   Working with Alignment Guides 106
   Creating New Alignment Guides 109
   Changing the Appearance of Alignment Guides 110

Grouping Objects **110**

Working with Graphics **111**
   Combining Images and Shapes 111
   Using Graphics and Text 114

6   Working with Backgrounds and Multimedia **117**

Changing Slide Backgrounds and Colors **118**
   Using the Slide Inspector to Change a Background 118
   Changing the Background by Combining Themes 120

Adding Visual Interest to Objects by Using the Opacity Setting **122**

Using Audio in a Presentation **127**
   Importing Audio Files 127
   Adding an Audio File to a Slide 128
   Using the Media Inspector to Adjust Audio Options 129

Using Video in a Presentation **131**

7   Managing Presentations **135**

Working with Keynote Views **136**
   Navigator View 136
   Outline View 137
   Slide Only View 137

Rearranging Slide Order **138**

Grouping Slides **140**

Skipping Slides While Viewing a Slideshow **143**

Working with Master Slides and Layouts **144**
Master Slide Options 145
Quick Access to Master Slides 148

Creating Speaker Notes **150**

Spell Checking and Find and Replace **151**
Using Spell Check 151
Using Find and Replace 152

8 Exploring
   Transitions and Builds **155**

Using Transitions Between Slides **156**
Choosing a Keynote Transition 158
Changing Transition Effects and Speed 159

What Are Builds? **160**
Getting Familiar with the Build Inspector 161
Text Builds 163
Table Builds 164
Chart Builds 165
Image Builds 168

Creating Multiple-Build Slides **168**

9 Viewing and Printing a Presentation **173**

Viewing a Slideshow **174**

Slideshow Viewing Preferences **175**

Creating a QuickTime Presentation **177**

Creating a PDF File of a Presentation **181**

Printing a Presentation **182**

Working with Presentation Hardware **184**

10 Extending Keynote **187**

   Creating New Themes **188**

     Selecting a Theme to Edit 188

     Choosing a Background and Graphics 190

     Editing Fonts and Styles 191

     Customizing Chart Types 192

     Saving a Custom Theme 193

   Creating New Master Slides **194**

   Keynote and Microsoft PowerPoint **196**

A Installing Keynote **199**

   Making Sure Your Mac Is Ready for Keynote **200**

   Installing Keynote **201**

B Keynote Keyboard Shortcuts **203**

C Helpful Keynote Web Sites **209**

Index **211**

About the Author

Curt Simmons is a popular author, technology trainer, and digital photo enthusiast. He has a bachelor's degree in speech communication and multiple computer industry certifications, and he is the author of more than 30 books about computer operating systems, networking, digital photography software, and more. When he is not writing, he spends his time with his wife and children and constantly working on his 100-year-old Victorian home.

Dedication

This one is for all of my public speaking teachers through the years, who taught me that the heart of any speech or presentation is always the message.

Acknowledgments

Thanks to Rick Kughen for giving me the green light on this book. Also, thanks to Brian Hubbard for the eagle eye and Laura Norman, Tonya Simpson, and Kitty Jarrett for their attention to the details. Finally, thanks to my family for their constant support.

We Want to Hear from You!

As the reader of this book, *you* are our most important critic and commentator. We value your opinion and want to know what we're doing right, what we could do better, what areas you'd like to see us publish in, and any other words of wisdom you're willing to pass our way.

As an associate publisher for Que, I welcome your comments. You can email or write me directly to let me know what you did or didn't like about this book—as well as what we can do to make our books better.

Please note that I cannot help you with technical problems related to the topic of this book. We do have a User Services group, however, where I will forward specific technical questions related to the book.

When you write, please be sure to include this book's title and author as well as your name, email address, and phone number. I will carefully review your comments and share them with the author and editors who worked on the book.

Email: feedback@quepublishing.com

Mail: Greg Wiegand
Associate Publisher
Que Publishing
800 East 96th Street
Indianapolis, IN 46240 USA

For more information about this book or another Que title, visit our Web site at www.quepublishing.com. Type the ISBN (excluding hyphens) or the title of a book in the Search field to find the page you're looking for.

INTRODUCTION

Ah, public speaking. You might prefer to call public speaking a "talk," a "presentation," or a "lecture," but let's face it: There is nothing in the world quite like having to stand in front a group of people and talk about something. There's nothing in the world that can produce the same mind-numbing fear and terror in most of us, either!

I don't want to start out on a bad note, but the truth of the matter is that public speaking is hard. It requires careful thought and preparation on your part, and then it requires effective delivery of the message. Those things don't happen by accident, as I'm sure you are quite aware, but there is certainly help for your public speaking engagements, and it comes in the form of a fine software package called Keynote.

Public Speaking—Then and Now

The following quick story is absolutely true, and it will help you gain an understanding of me, where I've come from in the public speaking world, and where things are today.

I grew up on a Texas farm, and as a teenager, I was heavily involved in 4-H. I frequently went to livestock shows and was involved in all the leadership activities that come along with 4-H; in fact, I was the local 4-H club president.

One summer, I attended a national livestock show, and the show included a public speaking contest. I was 17 at the time, and I had never given a speech in my life. I was primarily interested in the contest because of the $400 prize money, which isn't chump change for a high school student. So, I studied, I prepared, I practiced, and practiced, and practiced...you get the picture.

When the fateful day finally arrived, the contest was full of contenders—more than 100 of them. There were so many speakers that the contest ran all day and into the night. When I finally stood behind the podium to take my turn, it was shortly after midnight and there were only 5 people in the room. I was determined to give a good speech for the bleary-eyed judges, and that's what happened! I left the podium feeling good about the speech and happy I had entered.

Little did I know at the moment, I had done more than good. In fact, I had won the contest. When I found out the next day, I was ecstatic. However, I was told that the powers that be wanted me to present my speech at the show's closing banquet on Saturday night. No problem, right?

I arrived at the banquet and felt my heart sink into my toes. There were more than 900 people at the banquet, a large stage, and a spotlight on the podium where I would speak. This would be the second speech I had ever given, and I was terrified—to say the least!

The moral of the story is simply this: You probably have to give a speech, and you want Keynote to help you out. Maybe this is your first presentation, or maybe you are a pro. Regardless, public speaking has come a long way in our technologically advanced age, and presentation software like Keynote can be a great help!

Since my early days of speaking, I have given many speeches. In those early days, I didn't have the help of presentation software, but that has all changed. With presentation software, giving presentations is certainly easier, and one thing is for sure: Keynote has all the tools and features to help you prepare and deliver an excellent presentation.

Enter the World of Keynote

Keynote is presentation software that is designed to help you prepare a presentation and create graphics and slides that help convey your message to your audience members. Keynote—or any software, for that matter—is not the presenter; that job is up to you. Keynote is a speaker's aid to help you deliver your message.

I don't need to sell you on the virtues of Keynote. I'm sure you already own the software, or you wouldn't be reading this book. And yet, Keynote is a long-awaited and much-needed application for the Mac. Keynote is slick, fun, and easy to use, and it helps you create stunning and professional slides with little work. This is good news because it means you can spend more time working on your presentation rather than having to spend all your time fumbling with software.

Of course, Keynote isn't perfect. It's software, after all, and all software has some quirks and limitations. I'll point those out throughout the book and show you any quick workarounds you might want to use. Remember: Keynote works great and creates beautiful slides, so with the right approach, you can create stunning slides for every presentation.

How to Use This Book

I wrote this book so that it is easy to use; after all, you have enough to worry about in your life that you shouldn't have to try to figure out how to use a book that is supposed to help you! This book doesn't dwell on lofty ideas, such as world peace, and it doesn't ramble on about topics that are minor. In fact, every word in this book is important and can help you get the most out of Keynote.

This book is designed to make your life easier. As you look over the table of contents, you'll see that I have organized chapters in a logical way. To get started with Keynote and build a quick presentation, just check out Chapter 1, "Beginning Skills: Getting to Know Keynote." From there, the book explores topics with more depth so that you can build up your skills.

This book isn't a textbook or a novel. Each chapter stands on its own, and you should feel free to read the book from cover to cover or skip around and find out how to do tasks you need at the moment. This book is here to help you get Keynote to do what you want, so you can use the book in a way that works best for you.

I've included plenty of screen shots and step-by-step instructions to help you do things quickly. I've also included notes, tips, and cautions throughout. These side elements give you extra information that will make your work in Keynote easier and more efficient, so make sure you read them as you go. I don't explore every nook and cranny of Keynote, with pages of explanations and techno-babble; my job is to help you make Keynote work for you and do the things that you want.

This isn't a public speaking book, either, but it is difficult to talk about speaking and presentation software without talking about presentations themselves. Therefore, when appropriate, I give you some quick pointers about actually using the software when you speak. This information is extra, of course, but you'll find that your work with Keynote and your presentations with Keynote will be much better if you follow my advice.

I wrote this book because I love public speaking and I love software, like Keynote, that helps you and me do just that. If you have any questions, comments, or suggestions about the book, please don't hesitate to email me at curt_simmons@Hotmail.com or visit my Web site, www.curtsimmons.com. I'd love for you to stop by and say hello.

Are you ready to dig into the world of Keynote? I thought so, and Chapter 1 will get you started!

Conventions Used in This Book

I hope that this book is easy enough to figure out on its own, without requiring its own instruction manual. As you read through the pages, however, it helps to know precisely how I've presented specific types of information.

This book explains the essential concepts and tasks in an easily digestible format. Each chapter is loaded with visuals to help you follow procedures or just to help get a point across.

At the beginning of each chapter the *In This Chapter* list provides a framework for what you are about to learn. At the end of each chapter in *The Absolute Minimum*, you can review the main points covered in the chapter.

Web Page Addresses

Technically, a Web page address is supposed to start with `http://` (as in `http://www.curtsimmons.com`). Because Internet Explorer and other Web browsers automatically insert that piece of the address, however, you don't have to type it—and I haven't included it in the addresses in this book.

Special Elements

This book includes a few special elements that provide additional information not included in the basic text. These elements are designed to supplement the text to make your learning faster, easier, and more efficient.

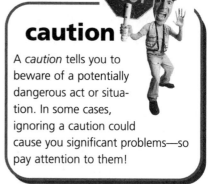

tip

A *tip* is a piece of advice—a little trick, actually—that helps you use your computer more effectively or maneuver around problems or limitations.

caution

A *caution* tells you to beware of a potentially dangerous act or situation. In some cases, ignoring a caution could cause you significant problems—so pay attention to them!

note

A *note* is designed to provide information that is generally useful but not specifically necessary for what you're doing at the moment. Some notes are like extended tips—interesting, but not essential.

IN THIS CHAPTER

- Learn what all those things on the Keynote screen mean

- Learn what fancy special effects—such as builds and transitions—can do to enhance even the lowliest of presentations

- Learn how to put together a basic presentation

- Learn where in this book to look next for creative inspiration

1

BEGINNING SKILLS: GETTING TO KNOW KEYNOTE

You need to make a presentation. Probably tomorrow. Your hands are sweating, you're nervous about getting your message across to your audience, and you have an overwhelming desire to ditch it all and go live in a remote mountain cabin, preferably one that's far from multimedia speakers, podiums, and corporate buzzwords such as *facilitate* or *utilizing*.

And on top of that, you have to use presentation software you are not familiar with. Relax. I'm here to help make that part easier. By the end of this chapter, you'll be able to get your thoughts onto a display screen without resorting to magic markers, and by the end of the book, you'll be a competent user of the program. Fair enough?

What Keynote Is All About

The truth is, you probably don't want to be a Keynote expert. You're already an expert lawyer, salesperson, college instructor, or whatever. That's enough.

You just want software to help you get your point across in your upcoming presentation. That's okay because that's exactly the purpose of Keynote: to help you create professional-quality presentations, using the power of Mac OS X without knocking your head against a wall.

In other words, you can look good with a minimum of effort. Keynote presentations let you include graphics, multimedia, text effects, and plenty of features that'll make your audience say, "Oh, *cool!*" And you'll accomplish it all with a few clicks. Really.

On the other hand, Keynote isn't perfect. As you'll discover in these pages, I'm not shy about enumerating its faults. I want you to use the software to get your work done, not spend hours cussing at it. Therefore, throughout this book, I point out the things that Keynote can't do as well as the things it can. And I tell you about the workarounds that can help you do what you need to, at least until Apple gets around to adding the feature. (That'll save you from looking for a feature that you think surely must be hidden in there, somewhere.)

Yet, overall, I think Keynote is a truly nifty program. It lets ordinary people—folks who don't want to be software experts—accomplish neat stuff without breaking into a sweat. Keynote may not be a Microsoft PowerPoint killer, but for sure it'll leave PowerPoint with a few nasty bruises.

I assume that you've already installed Keynote and you have it working. If you haven't done that already, see Appendix A, "Installing Keynote," for instructions. (Under most circumstances, you can just insert the CD-ROM and go, as with most Mac programs.)

This chapter covers the absolute least you need to know. You'll become familiar with the Keynote screen and what each of its components does.

Then you'll create a basic presentation that will let you get through the ordeal of tomorrow's presentation with all your hair intact. It won't be the most elegant presentation you'll ever do, but if you're on a short time line (or you want immediate gratification in getting this puppy working), this is the chapter for you: You will get the absolute basics out of the way by trying a follow-the-bouncing-ball tutorial. That way you can concentrate on the important things—like agonizing over what you'll say to convince the audience to sign on the nice dotted line.

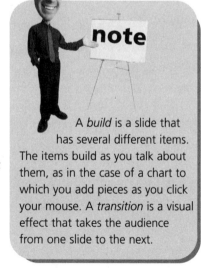

A *build* is a slide that has several different items. The items build as you talk about them, as in the case of a chart to which you add pieces as you click your mouse. A *transition* is a visual effect that takes the audience from one slide to the next.

This chapter also gives you a taste of a few spiffy Keynote features, such as builds and transitions. Even if you're in a rush to get the first presentation done, you'll probably want to include one of these just for fun, simply because Keynote is an incredibly fun application to use.

What Keynote Can Do

Before you start using Keynote yourself, let's take a moment to talk about what the software is capable of. When you shop for a new car, fitting the groceries in the trunk may be the real criterion for the model you take home, but it is fun to take the vehicle for a test drive. You might want to see if it really can go from 0 to 60mph in the time the company claims; even if yours is intended to be an around-town car, someday you might need that acceleration to reach highway passing speed.

So, start up Keynote. By default, the icon is in your Applications folder, but you might also have added it to the Mac OS X dock. When Keynote asks you to choose a theme, click **Close Document**. (You'll learn about themes in a few minutes.)

As soon as you have the Keynote screen in front of you, choose **File**, **Open Samples**. Keynote then shows a folder with a single file, Presentation Tips.key. Double-click the filename, and (eventually—this is a big file, so it may take a while) it starts up, looking something like what you see in Figure 1.1. Follow the onscreen instruction to click on **Play**, and you get a walk-through that shows you some of Keynote's reasons to brag.

FIGURE 1.1

Keynote includes a sample presentation that shows off some of its unique features.

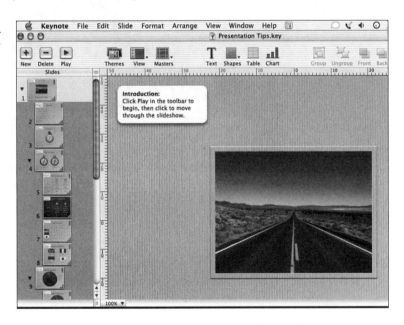

Don't close the sample document just yet. When you've walked all the way through the slideshow, you can use it to get familiar with the different parts of the Keynote screen.

Working with the Keynote Screen

The largest part of the Keynote application screen is the Slide Canvas, where you work with individual slides. On the Slide Canvas (as shown in Figure 1.2), you type text, insert graphics, create charts, and put together the content of your presentation.

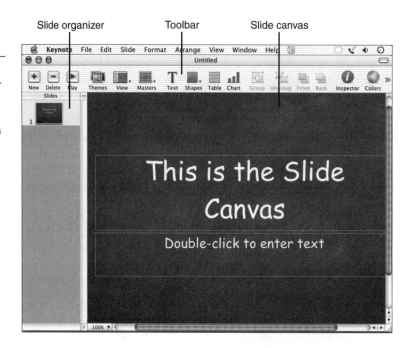

FIGURE 1.2

Keynote organizes the application with the Slide Organizer, a toolbar, and a working area called the Slide Canvas.

On the left side of the Keynote screen is the Slide Organizer, which lets you rearrange the order of your slides and move bullets from one slide to another. You can work with the Slide Organizer in two ways: in Navigator view, which shows thumbnail images of each slide, and in Outline view, where you focus on your presentation's text.

Using either view, you can indent slides so they follow your own particular form of organization or so they match your discussion outline.

Along the top of the Keynote screen is a toolbar. The toolbar makes it easy to change themes, views, and slide formats. From the toolbar, you can also add text, tables, charts, and graphic shapes, and you can modify colors and fonts.

Try out the toolbar by clicking **View** and then clicking **Show Notes**. Keynote adds a box at the bottom of the screen, into which you can type personal reminders of the points to cover—or whatever you feel like. The notes are just for you. The audience won't see them.

note

Most of the time, slide organization is simply a convenience, but organization can have other benefits. For instance, you can hide a set of slides so they won't be seen at show time. You'll learn more about this capability in Chapter 7, "Managing Presentations."

Introducing the Inspector

While you're looking at the toolbar, click **Inspector**. Keynote brings up a complex-looking, context-sensitive dialog box, called the Inspector, as shown in Figure 1.3. (*Context-sensitive* means that what you see in the Inspector changes based on the nature of the object you have selected.)

The Inspector also changes, depending on which Inspector that you select. Notice the different Inspector icons along the top of the window. You can click them to access different inspectors, depending on what you are working on. These are your options:

- **Slide Inspector**—This inspector allows you to manage major slide features, such as Master & Layout, Background, and Transition.
- **Graphic Inspector**—You manage graphics with this Inspector. You can use it to create fills, strokes, apply shadows, manage opacity, and much more.
- **Metrics Inspector**—You use this option to manage object location, size, width, and positioning.
- **Text Inspector**—You use this Inspector to manage text. You can use it to adjust the color, alignment, spacing, bullets, and numbering.
- **Build Inspector**—This Inspector allows you to create slide builds.
- **Table Inspector**—You can adjust the rows, columns, alignment, cell border, and cell background of your tables by using this Inspector.
- **Chart Inspector**—You can plot data, manage chart type and layout, and much more by using the Chart Inspector.
- **QuickTime Inspector**—You can use QuickTime movies on your slides with the QuickTime Inspector.

FIGURE 1.3

The Keynote
Inspector
organizes the
program's for-
matting controls
in one handy
little notebook.

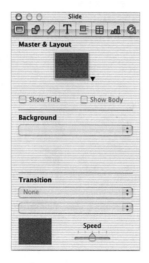

FIGURE 1.3

The Keynote
Inspector
organizes the
program's for-
matting controls
in one handy
little notebook.

This multilevel dialog box controls how objects look or behave. For instance, it's where you control the fonts or colors on a slide and where you adjust a chart's appearance. The Inspector can seem a little overwhelming at first, but I promise you it won't stay that way. You'll be using it often.

The Inspector gets less intimidating as you learn Keynote's formatting capabilities, as you'll do in Chapter 6, "Working with Backgrounds and Multimedia."

Creating Your First Presentation

Creating a Keynote presentation has only a few basic steps. Each step can get as complex as you want (or have time for), but it all comes down to this:

1. Select a theme
2. Design your slides
3. Organize the presentation
4. Save your work
5. Play the slideshow

We'll cover each of these steps briefly in the following sections and in more detail elsewhere in the book.

Ready? Start up Keynote (if it isn't running already), and you can create your first presentation.

Understanding Themes

A *theme* is simply a look that you apply to a presentation. When you choose a Keynote theme, you get an entire look, which includes everything from a color scheme to font settings to bullet styles. Best of all, themes are consistent across the set of slides you use (called *master slides*, which we'll get to in a moment), making your presentation look polished and visually well organized.

This is all the stuff you'd mess with for half an hour if you were trying to create your presentation in a word processor. The 12 themes that Keynote includes right out of the box are complete with textures and cut-outs for where your photos and illustrations will go.

Using themes makes it easy to select a mood for your presentation, whether it's a formal pinstripe-and-tie meeting or a casual overview for sharing information among team members.

The first thing Keynote requires you to do when you begin a new presentation is to choose a theme for the presentation. If you've just started up Keynote, it shows you the Choose a Theme window as its first action. If you played with the sample file earlier in this chapter, close it (you won't need it anymore) and then choose **File**, **New** to open the Choose a Theme window, shown in Figure 1.4. You just click a theme to select it.

FIGURE 1.4
Keynote practically insists that you start with a theme. The ones it includes are pretty nice.

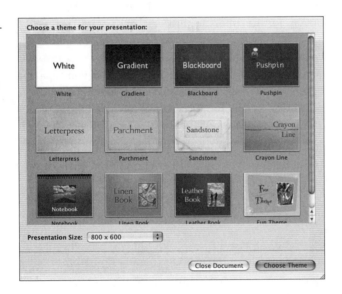

At the bottom of the Choose a Theme dialog box, you can choose a presentation size; this refers to the graphics resolution the program should use. Choose a presentation size that matches the screen resolution of the output display you expect to use. Newer projectors can handle 1024×768, and almost any projector can do

800×600. When in doubt, go with 800×600, which is Keynote's default anyway. If you're going to print your Keynote presentation instead of display it on a screen, the resolution won't matter as much.

For the purposes of this tutorial, leave the presentation size at the default value of 800×600.

Click **Choose Theme**. Keynote takes a few moments to build the template, and then it displays a title slide.

Introducing Master Slides

If you've used another presentation graphics application or a desktop publishing program, you might be familiar with master slides. In Keynote, as in other applications, a *master slide* is simply a predefined layout for a certain kind of content.

Granted, that sounds somewhat technical. What I mean is Keynote has already created nicely balanced layout pages for the different kinds of things you're likely to want to put on your slides. For instance, as you can see on your screen by now, Keynote starts out by displaying a title slide, which lets you type in a title and maybe a subtitle. There are several kinds of slides for the body of your presentation, such as Title & Bullets, in which the content pages are laid out for bulleted text on the left and a spot for a graphic on the right.

You'll learn more about master slides in Chapter 10, but for now the important thing to grasp is that master slides are the templates in each theme that make it easy to create slides that are known to look good.

> **note**
>
> You don't have to start from scratch. Keynote lets you import presentations from other documents, such as Microsoft PowerPoint and AppleWorks. It won't take much fiddling around for you to find the File, Import menu, but if you have several more-than-vanilla presentations, you'll want to check out Chapter 10, "Extending Keynote," which covers other document formats in detail.

Adding Text to a Slide

Right now, you're staring at a title slide. To add text, double-click in the text box, and you see a blinking cursor. Type. You probably figured that out pretty quickly.

Your slide might look something like the one in Figure 1.5.

Later, you'll learn to adjust text color, fonts, line spacing, and other formatting. You can play with the Inspector now—I'm sure you'll figure it out quickly enough without my help—but we'll cover all its options in later chapters.

FIGURE 1.5

Thanks to themes, a Keynote title slide looks pretty good with no help from you whatsoever.

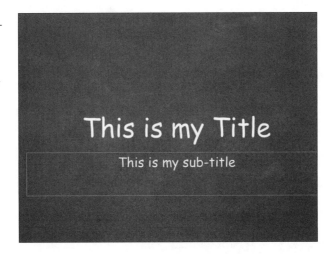

You don't have to have a title and a subtitle on your presentation. If you don't type anything in one of the spots where Keynote displays "double-click to edit," those spaces will appear as a blank space in your finished presentation.

Adding Slides

You can add a new slide to your presentation in one of three ways:

- Click the + in the Keynote toolbar (it says New underneath). If you do not see a toolbar, just select **View**, **Show Toolbar**.

- Choose **Slide** and then choose **New Slide** from the menu bar.

- Press **Shift+⌘+N**.

When you do any of these three things, you get another slide that uses the Title & Bullets layout. If you don't like that layout, you can choose another by clicking the **Masters** button in the toolbar; let's stick with the default Title & Bullets layout for now.

As with the title slide, this one lets you enter text simply by double-clicking in the predefined text box.

note

Keynote expects that you'll generally type into the text boxes it provides on the master slides, and most of the master slides expect you to be typing bullets rather than some other kind of text. For most uses, that's a reasonable expectation. However, you aren't constrained by this bullet-centricity. As you'll learn in Chapter 2, "Working with Text," you can always add a free text box, which isn't part of the master slide.

After you type each bullet, you press **Enter** (or **Return**, on some keyboards). Keynote automatically creates a new bullet and balances the spacing between the bullets. You can also create subsectioned bullets by pressing **Tab**.

Keynote doesn't try to second-guess your design style. If you try to fit 10 bullets on the page, the software will do its level best to accommodate you, even if the presentation gods would curse you for it. It won't *look* good when you do this, mind you, but Keynote will let you do it.

You could go on for hours, creating nothing but bulleted slides, and I'm sure many of your presentations do just fine with nothing else. (It's your brilliant message the audience is coming to hear, after all.) However, you didn't buy Keynote to create only plain-vanilla bullet slides, so read on.

Creating Tables in Slides

Ah! Here you'll finally get to play with something that makes Keynote special. Follow these steps to add a table to your presentation:

1. Choose **Slide**, **New Slide** to create a new slide.

2. From the Keynote toolbar, click the **Masters** button and choose **Blank**.

3. From the toolbar, choose **Table**. By default, Keynote creates a 3×3 grid (three rows and three columns) and brings up the Table Inspector; it also brings up the Chart Data Editor, which looks like a mini-spreadsheet.

4. Double-click a text box inside the table and then start typing. Keynote automatically formats the text so that it fits neatly inside each cell. Pressing Tab takes you to the next cell. Eventually, you'll end up with something like the table shown in Figure 1.6.

You can easily change the text alignment in a cell by selecting a whole column or single cell and then choosing a different alignment in the Table Inspector. Similarly, you can tell Keynote to align cells to the top or bottom.

tip

One of Keynote's delightful features is its ability to drop graphics inside tables, as well as change the cell background. In Chapter 3, "Using Tables," you'll learn how to make your tables look prettier.

FIGURE 1.6

Creating a basic
Keynote table
takes very little
time.

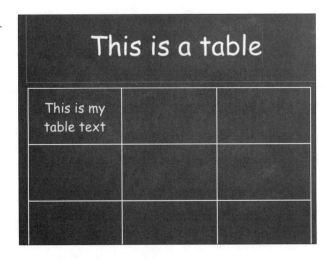

FIGURE 1.6

Creating a basic
Keynote table
takes very little
time.

Incorporating Charts in Slides

How about showing some numbers? To do so, you create another new slide (I find using the + in the Keynote toolbar the fastest way to do this), and from the **Masters** button on the toolbar, choose **Title Top**. Type a title if you like and then click **Chart** in the toolbar.

Poof! Keynote creates a sample chart on the slide for you, as shown in Figure 1.7. It also brings up the Chart Data Editor (a baby spreadsheet) and the Chart page of the Inspector.

FIGURE 1.7

When you create
a new chart in
Keynote, it sup-
plies a bit of
information to
get you started.

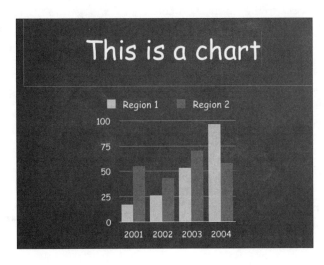

To get started with your chart, just type over the Region 1 and Region 2 data in the Chart Data Editor, filling in your own data, as I did in Figure 1.8. The Chart Data Editor works just like a spreadsheet, so you can add and delete columns and rows by using the buttons at the top of the dialog box. As you make changes, Keynote adjusts the graph. Note that if you do not enter any data for a column or row, Keynote simply does not display that column or row.

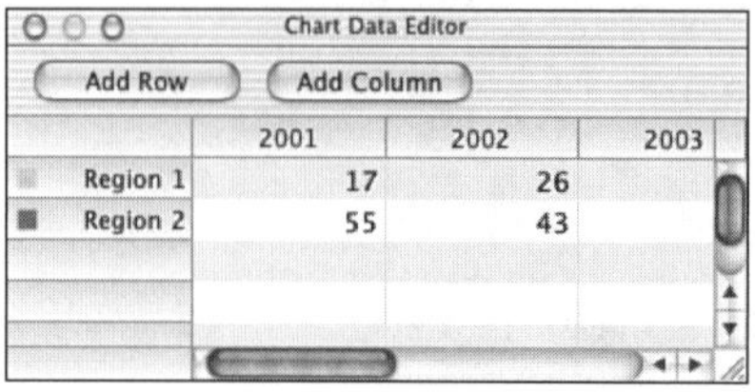

FIGURE 1.8

Keynote automatically adjusts the data in your chart as you make changes to the data.

		2001	2002	2003
	Region 1	17	26	
	Region 2	55	43	

Chart Data Editor — Add Row — Add Column

If the labels on your chart are too long, there are a couple ways to fix them. First, see if another chart type will look better; make sure the chart itself is selected in the Slide Canvas. Then, using the chart type drop-down in the Inspector, see how the different types work.

If they are still too long, you can change the orientation. With the chart still selected, choose **X-Axis** from the Inspector and then choose **Diagonal Labels**. The result is better but still too long; you need to shorten the text.

You need to go back to the Chart Data Editor. One way you can force labels to fit is to add a soft break in the title. Here's how:

1. Select the title.

2. Position the cursor in between the words you want to break.

3. Press **Option+Enter** to insert a soft break.

You'll learn how to make charts do what you want in Chapter 4, "Using Charts." For now, you have enough knowledge to move on to the next part of creating great presentation materials—adding graphics.

tip

Notice that I reminded you to ensure that the right object is selected on the Slide Canvas prior to selecting a menu? It may take you a little while to get into the habit of selecting something before you do something to it, but it's a habit you need to develop. Otherwise, you'll get frustrated by trying to get to a menu you *know* you've seen but that seems to have suddenly "disappeared."

Including Graphic Images in Slides

Keynote gives you several ways to add pictures and other graphic images to slides. And when you have images on a slide, there are several tools that let you add shadows, position images precisely where you want them, and scale and rotate them so that they look exactly as you envisioned them. You can use alignment guides, rulers, and positioning tags to make your graphics look more attractive. We'll cover these things in later chapters. For right now we're going to keep things simple.

I'll show you two ways to get images into Keynote. Just be aware that you'll learn more about this in Chapter 5, "Working with Graphics."

To add an image to your presentation, follow these steps:

1. Create another slide (by now you should have that + sign click down cold).

2. On the toolbar, choose the **Masters** button and then choose **Photo Horizontal**. Type a title, if you like, but the title is not what we're paying attention to here, so it doesn't really matter. Then click anyplace else on the slide.

3. Click the **Inspector** on the toolbar. On the Inspector, choose the **Slide Inspector** tab, which is the first tab at the top. The Inspector then says Master & Layout on top (see Figure 1.9).

Slide Inspector

FIGURE 1.9

The Slide Inspector enables you to choose some important slide options.

4. Under **Background** is a pull-down that says **Color Fill**. From that menu, choose **Image Fill**. Choose a graphic (in TIF, JPG, or almost any other file format) from somewhere on your system.

tip

If you don't have a photo gallery handy, the easiest spot from which to get pictures to play around with is the screen saver folder. From the **Finder**, look in the **Library Folder** and then **Desktop Pictures**.

Keynote stuffs your graphic into the box in the middle of the slide, as shown in Figure 1.10. Actually, it's covering the slide with the graphic and then laying a fat frame on top of it—rather the way you put a mat over a photo before you hang it on the wall.

FIGURE 1.10

Keynote makes sure your graphic fits in the frame.

Experiment with the Keynote master slides to see which layout works best for your images. You don't have to go way up to the toolbar on top; the same list appears on the Inspector, right above the background section you were just working with.

Perhaps you want to incorporate an image in a different part of the slide. This is no problem. Let's look at another way to include an image in your presentation, which will let you play with a few more features.

Create a new slide or just add the extra graphic to the current slide. Then follow these steps:

1. From the toolbar, choose **Shapes** and then click the circle. Keynote adds a small circle in the middle of the Slide Canvas.

2. Move the circle to another part of your screen. Notice that Keynote shows some positioning numbers as you do so. (We'll look at those in depth later on.)

tip

If you experiment with the graphic options, you might look for a way to crop the image—that is, show just one face in the crowd or a single leaf on a tree. If so, you'll discover a limitation of Keynote. You can't do cropping. To crop images, you need to use another application (such as iPhoto or Photoshop Elements) to manipulate the pictures before adding them to a slide.

3. Make sure your image is still selected, and then in the Inspector, click the **Graphic Inspector** tab, which is the second tab down—the one that looks like a circle and a square. Under **Fill**, choose **Image Fill** and, as you did a moment ago, choose the picture you want to display. Keynote displays the graphic inside the circle.

4. Experiment with **Scale to Fill**, **Scale to Fit**, **Stretch**, **Original Size**, and **Tile** to see how Keynote changes the way the picture displays.

Using this method to insert a graphic gives you more options, as shown in the edits I have made to Figure 1.11. You can do the following:

- Adjust the color and line weight around the image (Keynote calls it *stroke*) or have none at all.

- Change the *opacity*—the see-throughness—of the image so that anything that is already on the slide shows through the graphic.

- Add a drop shadow to the image, with a ridiculous number of adjustments (I mean ridiculous in a *nice* way, of course).

FIGURE 1.11

You can make a number of changes to your images by using Keynote.

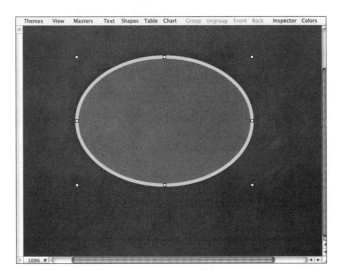

You still have the circle selected, right? With your mouse, grab a corner and twist it around to resize the image. You aren't stuck with an ordinary circle; you can change what started out as a circle into another shape.

Organizing Slides

No doubt, organization makes life much easier (yes, that includes your clothes closet). However, with a presentation, organization is of utmost importance. You want your audience members to walk away from your presentation with a clear understanding of the material you presented, and you want them to remember what you said.

The trick, along with having some good presentations skills, is simply organization. Keynote gives you a great way to organize your thoughts into slides and then organize those slides into a logical and meaningful presentation. The good news is that Keynote is very forgiving, meaning that you can organize, disorganize, and reorganize at will.

Choosing a View

As mentioned earlier in this chapter, you work with slides in the Slide Organizer, but the cool thing is that the Slide Organizer gives you two different views. The default view is Navigator view. In Navigator view, which you'll probably use most of the time, you see small slide icons representing each slide in your presentation. As you can see in Figure 1.12, if you click a slide in Navigator view, the slide appears on the Slide Canvas.

FIGURE 1.12

Navigator view contains your slides. You can click a slide on the left to see it in on the Slide Canvas.

Aside from the Navigator view, you can also use Outline view. To get to the Outline view, you select **View**, **Outline** (or you can more easily just click the **View** button on the toolbar and then click **Outline**). Outline view, as you can see in Figure 1.13, shows a small slide icon but is focused on giving you the text for each slide. It's...well...an outline!

FIGURE 1.13

You can use Outline view to get a quick look at your slide text.

Rearranging and Grouping Slides

So, how do you organize slides? Like most things on the Mac, the task is simple. You just drag slides around in either Navigator view or Outline view as needed to reorganize them. You can move slides around at any time or in any way simply by dragging them to the place you need them.

Aside from this easy way to shuffle slides, you can also group slides together for your own organizational purposes. As you can see in Figure 1.14, Slides 2, 3, 4, and 5 all reside under slide 1 and are shown indented. Note that this grouping doesn't mean anything for the presentation itself because the slides will be displayed in order, but the grouping feature can help you as you organize a presentation that has a lot of slides because it can help you keep the slides straight in your mind.

To group slides, you simply select the slide that you want to indent and press the **Tab** key, or you can just drag the slide slightly to the right in the left pane of the Organization view. The slide becomes indented, and the previous slide gets a triangle next to it. The slide will become indented and the slide it resides under gets a triangle next

tip

The grouping feature might seem a bit confusing at first, but just remember that the feature is there to help you, if you need it. If you don't need it, you don't have to use it. I usually don't use the grouping feature unless I am preparing a very long presentation with a lot slides. In those cases, the grouping feature helps cut down on slide confusion as I am working in Keynote.

to it to denote that it contains a group. Click the triangle to hide or show the slide grouping, as needed. You can group slides in any way that helps you. You can also move a group of slides to a new location in the Slide Organizer by simply dragging the first slide (the one with the triangle) to the new location. This action will move all the slides in the group.

FIGURE 1.14

Grouping is an organizational feature that helps you work on your presentation, but groupings do not affect the actual presentation.

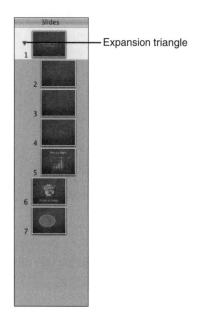

Expansion triangle

Playing the Slideshow

Ready to have a little fun? There is nothing more enjoyable in Keynote than getting to play your slideshow for the first time. After all, playing the slideshow is the culmination of your work!

The great news is that playing your slideshow is simple. Open the slideshow in Keynote if needed and then click the **Play** button on the toolbar. Or you can choose **View**, **Play Slideshow** if you like. Your Mac screen changes to display the slideshow full screen. Simply click your mouse to advance through the slideshow and press **Esc** on your keyboard when you are ready to leave the slideshow.

tip

If you want to see only part of the slideshow, in the Slide Organizer, select the slide you want to start with, and then click **Play** on the toolbar.

Saving Your Work

When you create a presentation, you need to make sure you save your work so that you can access the presentation anytime you want. When you save a presentation, all your slides and content are saved into one Keynote file. Depending on your needs, you might put that file on a disk or CD and carry it with you to the place where you will give your presentation, if you are not using your own laptop computer.

To save your work, just select **File**, **Save As**. A Save As dialog box (see Figure 1.15) appears. Give the presentation a name in the Save As text box and choose a place to save it in the Where text box (it goes to Documents by default). Also notice that this dialog box has the check box option "Copy movies into document." You use this feature if you put multimedia movies or sound files in your presentation (which you'll learn more about later). If you select this check box, the movies and sound files are saved as a part of your presentation. This feature allows you to use the presentation file on a different Mac and still see the movies or sound files.

FIGURE 1.15

You need to give your presentation a name and save location. If you are using movies or sound, consider copying those into the saved document.

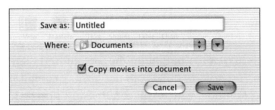

If you don't select the "Copy movies into document" check box, you can still use your presentation on your Mac (as long as you don't delete the movie or sound file), but if you transfer the Keynote file to a different Mac, the movies and sound will not appear in your presentation. As a safety measure, I always save my presentations so that the movies are copied into the document, just in case.

Introducing Builds

Let's say you are giving a presentation about last month's sales at your company. You could use a pie chart, but wouldn't it be cool if individual pieces of the pie could fly onto the screen and fit together as you talk about them? Well, you can make this happen!

The process of animating slides is called *builds*, and it simply means that you select different items on a slide and apply a build style to them. When the slide first appears, you can click to have individual build elements appear on the slide when you need them.

You can use builds with a number of different Keynote features. Builds have three major uses that you should keep in mind:

- **To animate slides**—Animation provides visual interest and helps stimulate the audience's attention. A build is a like a nice cup of coffee during your presentation.

- **To disclose content in pieces**—One of the great benefits of builds is they enable you to disclose pieces of content on a slide in different pieces. Going back to our pie chart example, you can have each piece of the pie appear on the screen as you talk about it, rather than showing the audience the entire pie chart at one time. This helps keep your audience focused on what you are talking about at the moment.

- **To show relationships**—Because builds can introduce pieces of slide content as needed, using builds is a great way to show relationships between different items on a slide.

To create a build, you choose the slide you want to work on and use the Build Inspector by clicking the **Inspector** button on the toolbar and then clicking **Build Inspector**, as shown in Figure 1.16. Builds are not terribly complicated, but they deserve some careful explanation, which you can find in Chapter 8, "Exploring Transitions and Builds."

FIGURE 1.16

Builds, which you create with the Build Inspector, give you a fun way to animate slides and control slide content.

Introducing Transitions

Transitions are simply graphic elements that move a presentation from one slide to the next. First of all, you don't have to use any transitions in your presentation if you don't want to. When you simply click your mouse during a presentation, one slide will disappear, and the next will appear. However, if you want to add a bit of flare and visual interest to a presentation, you should consider using transitions between slides.

Keynote gives you several cool and smooth transitions, such as a cube effect, slide flip, mosaic, drop, twirl, and so forth. The good news is that you can easily select a transition for a slide and even adjust the speed of the transition to match the mood and speed of your presentation.

Once again, transitions are optional, but they do give a graphic flare to your presentation. You can learn more about using them in Chapter 8.

THE ABSOLUTE MINIMUM

When you need to put a Keynote presentation together in a hurry, just keep these tips in mind:

- Keynote provides you with a simple interface. Use the screen to work on your slides, the Slide Organizer to keep everything in order, the Inspector to access different controls and features, and the toolbar and menu options to get to Keynote features.

- To create a basic presentation, first choose a theme. Next, enter text, charts, tables, and photos, as needed, on your slides. Add more slides as necessary and organize them by using the Slide Organizer. Use the Play function to see your presentation. Make sure you save your presentation.

- Keynote is capable of advanced presentation features that are easy on your brain. You can make charts and graphs, work with multimedia, create slide builds, use transitions, and much more!

IN THIS CHAPTER

- Create and edit text on Keynote slides
- Learn to use a variety of fonts to add interest to presentations
- Work with spacing, bullets, and numbering for a more professional look
- Make text work in your presentation for a variety of purposes

2

WORKING WITH TEXT

Let's face it: For all the bells and whistles Keynote (or any other presentation software, for that matter) provides, the crux of any presentation is the text that the audience sees on the slides. After all, the purpose of any presentation, regardless of the type, is to provide information to audience members. Without that information, your presentation has no meat. It's like having a small appetizer and no meal.

The Truth About Presentation Text

Obviously, it's more fun to work with graphics and photos than with text in a program like Keynote, and that's fine. We'll get to graphics in upcoming chapters, but before you get carried away with the cool features of Keynote, you need to stop and think about what you want to say in your presentation. From there, you can build the text for your slides and make your presentation great.

Before we get into the Keynote interface and start working with text, let's consider a few truths about text on slides. No, this information isn't in Keynote, but it comes from someone who has used Keynote and other similar applications for presentations and who knows a thing or two about presentations.

All too often, speakers and presenters end up using presentation software, such as Keynote, as a crutch. In other words, the slides actually become the presentation, and the speaker becomes someone who "helps" the slides. In reality, the slides should simply be a visual aid for a presentation. You should use slides to help convey your message, point out important issues, or show graphics that help explain what you are talking about. The slides you use should back up what you are saying: The slides shouldn't be the presentation itself, with you making a few comments here and there. Don't let your slides take over! You are the presenter, so stay in charge and make your slides work for you.

With that thought in mind, then, what are some things you should do when you create text for slides? There are few important ideas to keep in mind, and the following sections highlight those ideas.

> **tip**
>
> You should know what you want to say in your presentation before you come to Keynote to develop your presentation. Your best starting point may still be the old pencil and paper!

Make the Text Easy to Read

As a Keynote user, you have a lot of different font and text style options available to you. In fact, you can make any text look just about any way that you want, and you'll see how later in this chapter. At this point, however, the main question you need to ask yourself is, "Should I?" Just because Keynote gives you a bunch of text and font style options doesn't mean that you should try to use all of them. The available options are there to give you the flexibility you need when you create a presentation, but all text is not created equal. In fact, many text fonts and styles are entertaining but difficult to read. For example, take a look at Figure 2.1.

FIGURE 2.1

This Keynote text is clear and easy to read.

FIGURE 2.1

This Keynote text is clear and easy to read.

Notice that the text on this slide is easy to read. The text option you see here comes directly from one of the theme templates, and I have not modified it in any way. Now, take a look at Figure 2.2.

FIGURE 2.2

This Keynote text looks cool, but it may be difficult for audience members to read.

This text also comes directly from a theme. It looks cool, but the problem is that the text may be difficult for audience members to read.

As you are planning text, think carefully about the presentation. You want your slides easy to read and easy to understand. If someone has to stare at the slide for a moment to decipher the text, that is a moment he or she is trying to understand your slide and not listening to you. You should choose text that is quickly and easily readable. Sure, you can use interesting or odd text as needed, but always think in terms of readability, and as the old adage goes, "better safe than sorry."

Keep It Short

Slide text should be used to present bursts of information—ideas the audience can quickly read and remember. Think of it this way: If audience members are taking notes, what do you really want them to remember? This guiding question will help you create great slide text every time. As you are writing text, make sure you keep it short. For example, take a look at the slide in Figure 2.3.

FIGURE 2.3

There is too much information on this slide.

As you can see, this slide has too much information. If you start creating a paragraph of text on a slide, that should be a warning sign to you. Audience members will pause and read the slide, ignoring you as they do. Also, from a distance, a paragraph of text is difficult to read. Sure, you can use a paragraph if absolutely necessary, but just remember that paragraphs of text on slides do not work well and greatly slow down your presentation. Figure 2.4 shows the same information as Figure 2.3 but presents it in a bullet-point format.

As you can see, the bullet-point text conveys the same information as the paragraph text, is easy and quick to read, and keeps the audience's attention focused on you, the speaker!

FIGURE 2.4

This bullet-point text is quick and easy to read.

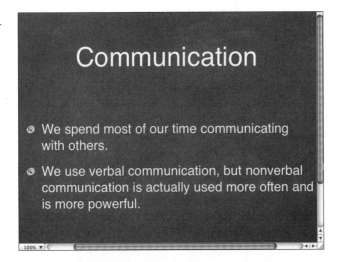

Keep It Simple

Consider these two sentences:

- Due to kinesic communication behavior, a public speaker may inadvertently display nonverbal communication cues.
- Body language has a great impact on what you say.

These sentences say exactly the same thing. *Kinesic communication* refers to communication of the body, or nonverbal communication, and it has a great impact on what a public speaker says. Now, imagine these statements on a slide. Which one would work best?

The point is simply this: The information that you put on your slides should be simple and clear. Audience members should not have to grapple with the meaning of the text on a slide. Make the slide text clear and then feel free to add information about the text as you talk with your audience. Your audience has the job of understanding your message, so don't make the audience's job more difficult than necessary!

Highlight Main Ideas

As you prepare slide text, think carefully about what you want the text to say; make every word count. Your best bet is to always think in terms of main ideas. Following is an example of information you might want to convey to an audience:

> This year, with the release of new products, we are expecting to see a thirty percent increase in domestic sales, a twenty percent increase in foreign sales, and a staggering sixty percent increase in Internet sales. This upturn in sales is good news for all of us. Since most of us have some kind of profit sharing attached to our base pay, we'll all make more money this year!

What are the main ideas you could pull out on a slide? As you might guess, your slide could look something like the example in Figure 2.5.

FIGURE 2.5

You can easily pull out the main ideas for your audience's consideration.

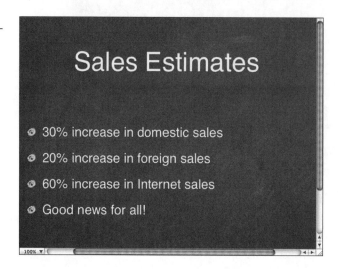

The object here is to highlight the main ideas on the slide. As you talk about the main ideas, you can add any necessary details you like, but you should keep the slide focused on the main ideas. Ask yourself "What do I really want my audience members to know?" when you create your slide text. This will help you scale down your text to the main points.

Watch Your Spelling and Punctuation

First things first: You are not writing a formal paper for a Composition 101 class when you create text for your slides. You are free to use incomplete sentences as needed, which is often the case when you use bullet points. As long as the bullet points are easy to read and make sense, you're in good shape.

tip

In a technology world, most presenters seem to go overboard with information. Your best approach is to always keep things simple and understandable. You want your audience to leave knowing what you said, not that you said so much it was confusing!

However, this doesn't mean you can ignore every rule in the English language either. You need to be careful to watch your spelling and comma usage and make sure you use periods where they are needed. Mistakes on Keynote slides make you look unprepared, so give your slides a thorough editing. It is also a good idea to have someone else read your slide text for common usage and punctuation errors.

Don't Overcrowd

When you create Keynote slides, you might have a tendency to overcrowd the slides with text in order to use fewer slides. Keynote lets you be the boss, and it lets you put a lot of text on a slide, but please don't. Always use more slides instead of crowding text onto slides. When you think about text, try to keep each individual slide to a heading and a few bullet points or other chunks of text. Your audience should be able to read your slide in a few moments.

Entering Text on Slides

After you have chosen a theme and decided on the text you want to show, you are ready to enter the text on your slides. The good news is that Keynote attempts to help you by giving you slide templates and styles to work with. If you are happy with what you see, all you have to do is double-click the text and type over it (see Figure 2.6). It doesn't get any easier than this. Using the provided text boxes, you simply enter your own text, and you get a smooth-looking presentation without any hard work.

> ### tip
>
> Everyone loves a good joke or pun, but jokes and puns are often best left said instead of written on a slide. For some reason, jokes and puns on slides often do not come across well. I'm not saying that you can't use them in a presentation; you just need to be wary when you do. Cartoons often work well on slides, but you need to make sure you are not violating any copyright laws and that any cartoon you decide to use is appropriate and comes off well.

FIGURE 2.6
You double-click to enter your text.

After you create the slide title page, click the **New** button on the toolbar to move to the next slide. The next slide you see is a content slide, as shown in Figure 2.7. It has a title field and generally a place to type bullets, depending on the template you have chosen to work with.

FIGURE 2.7

Most content slides give you a title option and a bulleted list where you can enter text.

To type bullet points, just type your text and press the **Enter** (or **Return**) key. This will move you down a line and give you another bullet point. As you can see, the text feature in Keynote works similarly to a basic word processing program.

If you need to change or edit any text you have already typed, just click where you need to make the change, and the cursor will move to that location. Then you simply fix the text as needed.

Deleting a Text Box

What do you do if a slide gives you a text box that you don't need? For example, let's say you are using a template, and a slide gives you a title and a field for text. However, you don't want to use text on the slide, but you want to insert a photograph (which you'll learn more about in Chapter 5, "Working with Graphics"). No problem. You can lose the text box. Click it one time, and little boxes appear around the outside of the box, as shown in Figure 2.8. These boxes are called *selection handles*, and they give you control over the text box, graphic, table, chart, and anything else that you select. Simply press the **Delete** key, and the box disappears.

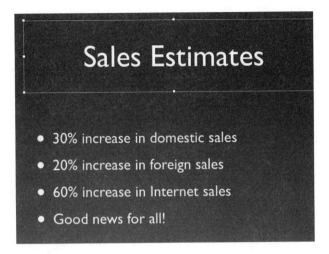

Adding a Text Box

What if you need to add a text box to a slide? No problem. Just click the **Text** button on the toolbar, and a new text box appears on the Slide Canvas. You can drag the text box around so that it is placed where you need it, or you can simply double-click inside the box and start typing your text. You can also expand the text box so that the text is centered on the slide by dragging the handles at either end of the box, as shown in Figure 2.9. As you can see, Keynote is rather versatile and easy to work with!

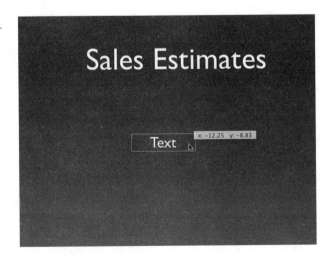

Working with Fonts and Styles

Fonts, also called *typefaces*, are a lot fun to work with because they allow you to customize your presentation and make the font look exactly as you like. You aren't stuck with the font that accompanies the template you selected.

To change a font, just select the text you want to change (or just click inside the text box to change it all) and select **Format**, **Font**, **Show Fonts**. As you can see in Figure 2.10, the Font dialog box that appears is the same thing you see in Mac OS X. All you have to do is select the font you want to use and change the size if necessary.

FIGURE 2.10

You can use the Font dialog box to select a different font.

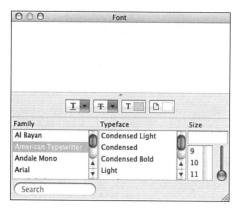

What fonts should you use? That is entirely up to you and the needs of your presentation, but here are a few pointers. First, serif fonts, such as Times New Roman, Baskerville, New York, and Palatino, work great for titles. They have a formal feeling and are easy to read. For a less formal approach and for bullet or body text, sans serif fonts, such as Arial, Tahoma, and Optima, all work great. You don't need to memorize font types in order to make a good selection; just let your eyes guide you. Choose a font and take a critical look at the text. Then ask yourself if the style works well with your discussion and if the font is easy to read. Some fonts have a lot of curly-cues and other features that may take up more room on your slide, so take that issue into consideration as well.

To use the Font dialog box, you simply choose a font family, a typeface, and a size. First, you use the scrollbar and under the Family category to choose a font family, such as Arial, Helvetica, or Baskerville. Depending on the family you choose, you might have some Typeface options. The Typeface options determine how the font looks, such as condensed, light, bold, regular, and so on. The options differ, depending on the font. Simply scroll through the Typeface list of options and select anything you like. Next, under Size category, scroll through the size list and select the font size that you want to use.

Notice that above the Family, Typeface, and Size options are drop-down menus for Spacing (the options are none, single, double, and color), Text Strikethrough (the options are none, single, double, and color), Text Color (if you click this option, the Colors dialog box appears), and Document Color (if you click this button, the Colors dialog box appears). As you can see, you simply click your way to the fonts and styles that you want.

Now, there are some extras on the Font dialog box that I want to point out, simply because you'll probably find some of the features useful. Click the **Action** drop-down menu (the button that looks like a wheel or gear in the lower-left corner of the Font dialog box, next to the Add [+] and Delete [-] buttons) to access the menu (see Figure 2.11).

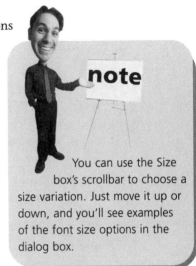

note

You can use the Size box's scrollbar to choose a size variation. Just move it up or down, and you'll see examples of the font size options in the dialog box.

FIGURE 2.11

The Action menu provides access to additional options when you're working with fonts.

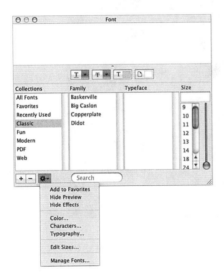

The following options are available:

- ■ **Add to Favorites**—This option adds the font selection to your favorites list.
- ■ **Show/Hide Preview**—I like this option because it shows a preview of the font in the Font dialog box. This way, you can see exactly how the font will look before you apply it to your text. You can also choose to hide this option if you do not want to see a preview.

- ■ **Show/Hide Effects**—This feature allows you to see or not see effects that you add to fonts, such as shadowing, color, and so on.
- ■ **Color**—The Color option opens the Colors dialog box so you can change the color of your text. See the next section, "Using the Text Inspector," for more details about working with color.
- ■ **Characters**—This allows you to see characters that you can insert into text, such as math characters, stars, arrows, and a host of others.
- ■ **Edit Sizes**—This feature allows you to edit the default slider list of font sizes and even enter new sizes and create fixed size lists.
- ■ **Manage Fonts**—This option takes you to the Internet, where you can find more fonts and download them to your computer.

As you are thinking about fonts, it is important not to get "font happy." For example, take a look at Figure 2.12.

FIGURE 2.12

Using too many fonts on the same slide does not look good.

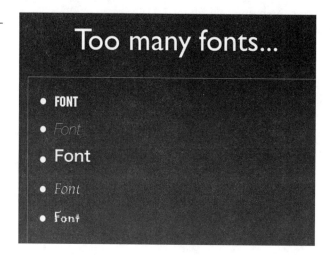

Have you ever visited a Web site that looked like the author tried to use every Web graphic in the world? I thought so. You can get into the same kind of trouble with Keynote fonts. Just because you can use multiple fonts on a slide doesn't mean that you should. Sure, feel free to mix fonts, but always ask yourself why you're doing so. Contrasting fonts work well to highlight certain ideas, but for the most part, your slides will be easiest to read if you stick to the same font. Avoid using different fonts excessively because that makes slides start to look comical and detracts from their content.

Using the Text Inspector

You can use the Text Inspector to manage text quickly and easily. Like most things in Keynote, the Inspector gives you some helpful features and quick options for working with text. You can access the Text Inspector by first selecting some text on a slide and then clicking the **Inspector** icon on your toolbar. As you can see in Figure 2.13, the Text Inspector gives you a few helpful options. The following sections explore these features.

FIGURE 2.13

The Text Inspector gives you quick and helpful options.

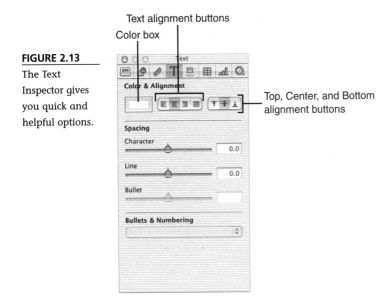

Text alignment buttons

Color box

Top, Center, and Bottom alignment buttons

Changing Text Color

Keynote doesn't keep you tied to the same text color that the theme provides. In fact, you can easily change the text color to anything you want. The Colors dialog box gives you several options for quickly selecting color (see Figure 2.14). First, you can choose a color by simply clicking the color wheel. If you don't like using the wheel, you can choose to use the color sliders, color palettes, image palettes, or crayons. These variations simply give you more options for selecting color. Also, notice the Opacity slider at the bottom of the dialog box. The *opacity* of a color refers to how transparent the color appears. The higher the opacity setting, the darker or brighter the color appears. The lower the opacity setting, the lighter or more transparent the color appears. This feature allows you to increase or decrease the opacity of a base color to effectively get the color shade that you want.

FIGURE 2.14

The Colors dialog box allows you to change the color of text.

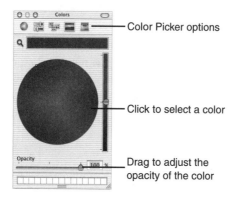

Color Picker options

Click to select a color

Drag to adjust the opacity of the color

To change the color of text, follow these steps:

1. Select the text and then click the **Inspector** button on the toolbar.

2. Click the **color box** on the Text Inspector, which opens the Colors dialog box, as shown in Figure 2.14. Or, you can just click the **Colors** button on the Keynote toolbar.

3. Click a **color picker** option at the top of the Colors dialog and then select a color. In Figure 2.14, the color wheel is selected. Simply click a color on the wheel to apply it to your text.

4. Drag the slider to adjust the opacity of the color as needed.

5. Take a look at the opacity on the slide. If you like what you see, close the Text Inspector. If not, go back to the Text Inspector and adjust the opacity again.

As you can see, changing text's color is quick and easy, but you need to make sure the text color you choose looks good and matches with the theme you are using. The color should contrast against any background colors or graphics so that audience members can easily read the text. White text on a black background or black text on a white background is always safe. Be careful with combinations such as pale yellow on a gray background.

Managing Text Alignment and Spacing

You can use the Text Inspector to align text in a text box. Keep in mind that when you work with text, alignment and even spacing are maintained within the text box. Therefore, if you choose a left-justified alignment, the text is left-justified within the text box where it resides.

You can easily change the alignment of text by selecting the text and accessing the Text Inspector. Then you can choose an alignment option by clicking a provided button (refer to Figure 2.14). You can choose left alignment, center, right alignment, or block alignment. You can also choose to align the top, center, or bottom of the text box. This feature can be particularly helpful with titles. For example, take a look at Figure 2.15.

FIGURE 2.15
Keynote provides several helpful text alignment options.

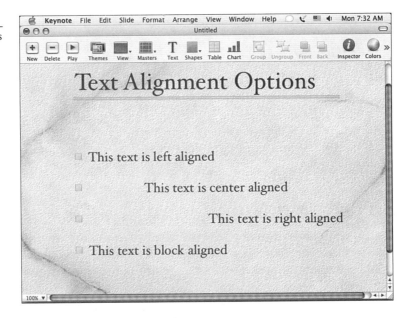

For the most part, the left alignment option is the best choice. After all, most text that we read is left-aligned. So when might you use the other options? That all depends on the slide. As you work with different slides, you might include both text and graphics text and tables or charts. In this case, you might work with text that needs to fit into a certain area or look a certain way to match up with other slide elements. In this case, the alignment options may help you because you can justify the text within the text box in a way that looks best on the slide.

In the center of the Text Inspector are some helpful spacing options. Select the text you want to change and use the **Character**, **Line**, and **Bullet** slider bars to adjust the spacing of text that appears between characters, lines, and bullets, respectively. As you can see in Figure 2.16, I have changed the character alignment to make the title characters spread out.

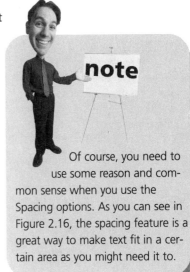

Of course, you need to use some reason and common sense when you use the Spacing options. As you can see in Figure 2.16, the spacing feature is a great way to make text fit in a certain area as you might need it to.

FIGURE 2.16

You can use the Spacing options in the Text Inspector to adjust the space between characters, lines, and bullets.

Using Bullets and Numbering

Bullets and numbering are a key part of most slides that have text. In fact, most information that you choose to put in text form in a presentation uses a bullet or number format. The simple fact is that bullets and numbers are easier for people to read and remember.

When you choose to use bullet text, Keynote provides you with a default bullet or number list. However, you can make some changes to the bullets or numbers by using the Text Inspector. If you select a bulleted or numbered list and then click the **Inspector** button on the toolbar to open the Text Inspector, you see the Text Inspector, as shown in Figure 2.17.

FIGURE 2.17

You can adjust bullets and numbering on the Text Inspector.

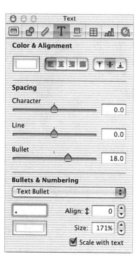

Notice, first of all, that the Text Inspector has a drop-down menu where you can choose Text Bullet, Number, Custom Image, Image Bullet, or None. However, you might want to use a custom bullet, such as a GIF or JPEG image you have downloaded from the Internet or that you have in another graphics program. Keynote gives you a lot of flexibility with bullets and numbers.

Notice also that you can align the bullets and numbers to move them up and down as needed so that they align correctly with the text. Also, you can adjust the size of the bullets or numbers by using the spinners next to the Size field or by typing in a new size. You can change the color of the bullets or numbers by using the Color box. Just click the **Color** box, and you'll see the Colors dialog box once again. Finally, the Scale with Text check box is selected by default so that Keynote can try to keep the bullets or numbers from overwhelming the text.

If all this sounds a bit overwhelming, just keep in mind that these options are provided to give you the extreme flexibility you want. You don't have to actually use any of them, but the point is that you can adjust the bullets and numbering in just about anyway that you like.

Let's take a look at an example. The following steps show you how to use a custom image as a bullet:

1. In Keynote, click the **New** button to create a new slide.
2. Click the **Masters** drop-down menu and choose the **Title & Bullets** master.
3. On the slide, type the first bullet and then click the **Inspector** button on the toolbar.
4. Choose the **Text Inspector**, and under **Bullets and Numbering**, choose the **Custom Image** option.
5. Click the **Choose** button at the bottom of the Text Inspector and then browse your computer to choose any image file. A picture file will work nicely.
6. Select the image file you want and click **Open**. The picture now appears on your slide as a bullet, and each bullet you add to this slide will also use the image (see Figure 2.18). Very cool!

As is often the case in Keynote, you have a lot of options, but be wary of overdoing it with bullets and numbers. The image bullet options can be a lot of fun, as you can see in Figure 2.19, but be careful. In the end, bullets and numbers are just organizational features, and you shouldn't liven them up so much that they get more attention than the text or other graphic on your slide. You need to take a hard look at the bullets and numbers and make sure they fit with the style of your slide and, of course, exercise some common sense.

FIGURE 2.18

Using a photo to
create a bullet
can add some
visual interest to
a slide and keep
your audience
focused on your
material.

FIGURE 2.19

Image bullets
can add a lot of
flash to your
slide, but use
them with care
so you don't
overwhelm your
text.

Setting Text Tabs

By default, each theme is preset with its own text tabs. Text aligns and falls based on you pressing the Tab key and entering that text. However, if you want to change the text tabs, you can do that easily in order to make the slide look the way you want. In Keynote, click **View**, **Show Rulers**. This turns on the Rulers features, as you can see in Figure 2.20. You can see the text tab marks on the top ruler. Simply move the slider arrows to adjust the tabs as necessary. If you want to adjust only one line of text, select it first and then use the slider arrows.

FIGURE 2.20

You can use the ruler to change the text tabs as needed.

Importing Text

You may have already created text in a word processing program that you would like to import into Keynote. Due to the nature of slides in Keynote, you can't directly import text. You can, however, copy and paste text from any other Mac application, and you can directly import PowerPoint presentations into Keynote. See Chapter 9, "Viewing and Printing a Presentation," to learn more about importing PowerPoint presentations.

tip

If you get text tab happy and foul everything up, don't worry: You can go back to the theme's defaults easily. Just click **Format**, **Reapply Master to Selection**. This, however, will also change the bullet styles and font settings back to those of the master theme as well.

The Absolute Minimum

When you are working with text in Keynote, just keep these tips in mind:

- Think and plan carefully when you insert text. Remember that text is the main point of your slides, so think about what the text conveys. Keep your text short, simple, and to the point. Audience members most easily remember short bursts of information.

- Themes provide you with standard text boxes that you simply double-click to enter text.

- Use the Text Inspector to adjust text colors, alignment, spacing, and bullets and numbers. Use the Font dialog box to make changes to fonts and the Colors dialog box to add color to text.

IN THIS CHAPTER

- Create tables that make your content clear
- Format and use table content
- Make tables look the way you want
- Work with cells, rows, and columns to make your information shine

3

USING TABLES

Tables, along with charts, which we will explore in Chapter 4, "Using Charts," are mainstays of presentation. After all, a table can be a great way to show your audience members information and help them understand some concept or idea you are trying to get across.

The good news is that you won't have to spend a lot of sweat and tears with tables in Keynote. As with most things in Keynote, the software does most of the hard work for you so that you can focus on your presentation's content. In this chapter you'll learn how to create, customize, and manage tables in presentations.

The Wonderful World of Tables

Okay, maybe tables aren't like flashy graphics or cool multimedia that will dazzle your audience, but let's also face the facts: Depending on the kind of presentation you are tackling, tables can be very helpful in a number of ways. The purpose of a table is to display information to your audience. The table gives the audience members an organized, systematic look at some content you are presenting, and in reality, content presented as a table is easier than text information for audience members to remember later because it gives what might be boring content a visual impact. For example, take a look at the table in Figure 3.1.

FIGURE 3.1

Tables present information in a clear and concise manner.

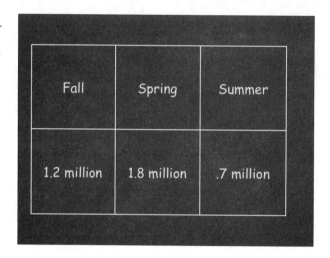

This table takes a simple three-column and two-row approach that gives sales figures for different periods of the year. The table is very basic in nature, but it makes otherwise bland information more interesting and easy to understand. You could jazz this table up a bit by using more colors and even marking the low period (summer) in red or using a graphic, which you'll see how to do later in this chapter.

When should you use a table? Here are some quick tips to remember:

- **Use tables to present numbers and figures**—The table format naturally lends itself to numbers and figures and keeps audience members from getting lost in a jumble of numeric information. If you use numbers and figures in a presentation, you should think in terms of tables.

- **Use tables to show contrasting information**—Tables work great when you have different pieces of information that fit together or contrast in some way. The table format helps show relationships between pieces of data in a memorable way.

■ **Use tables to show time line issues**—If you are talking about different periods of the year or even periods of different years, you can use a table to show the information. Tables can help audience members establish a mental time line that gives greater meaning to information.

Can you overuse tables? Sure. As with any presentation element, you should question yourself if you have table after table in your presentation. Use tables when needed, but use them sparingly, or they start to lose their impact. Keep it simple, keep it clear, and make sure the table has a solid purpose before using it in your presentation.

Creating a Table

You can create a new table on a slide by following these steps:

1. Click the **New** button to create a new slide.

2. Click the **Masters** button on the toolbar and choose the **Blank master**.

3. Click the **Table** icon on the Keynote toolbar or select **Edit**, **Place**, **Table**. The table appears on the slide canvas, and the Table Inspector opens, as shown in Figure 3.2. Notice that, by default, Keynote creates a 3×3 table.

FIGURE 3.2

A simple table is inserted, and the Table Inspector appears.

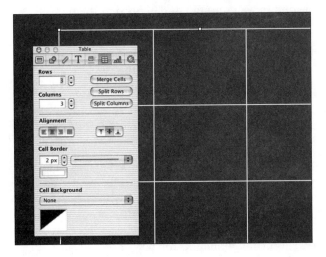

You can resize the table by using the selection handles. Simply drag them to shrink, enlarge, or resize the table in any fashion that you want (see Figure 3.3). You can also move the entire table around by positioning your mouse anywhere on the table (except the selection handles) and dragging.

FIGURE 3.3

You can resize
and move a
table as needed.

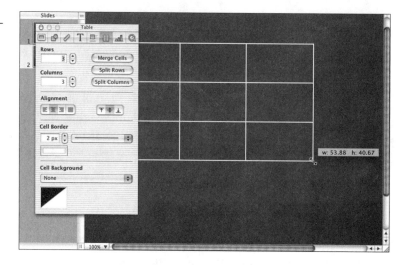

Moving Around in a Table

You can easily move around in a table in a few different ways, depending on what you want to do. First of all, keep in mind that you can select the entire table by clicking outside the table and then clicking the table one time. This allows you to resize the table and move it around as described in the previous section.

You can also move around in the individual cells within the table. Here's how:

1. Click outside the table and then click the table to select it.

2. Click the desired cell. Yellow highlight appears around the cell's border so that you know the cell is selected.

3. When a cell is selected, press the arrow keys on your keyboard to move from cell to cell.

You can also select cell borders and adjust them as you like. Just select the cell and then click the desired border. This action highlights the border so you can drag it as needed to change your table, as shown in Figure 3.4.

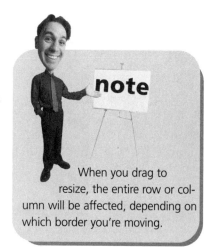

When you drag to resize, the entire row or column will be affected, depending on which border you're moving.

Drag to resize

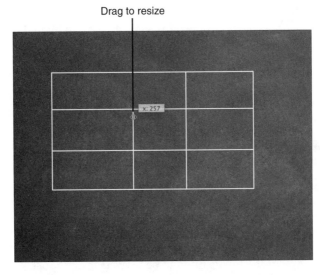

Entering and Formatting Text

Tables are designed to hold information, primarily text that describes the content of
the table. After all, it is data that is on display—the table is essentially an organizational method that makes the data easier to read and understand. Therefore, you
need to enter text in a table, make it fit, and make it look the way you want it to
look (and in a way that makes it easy to read).

First things first: You can easily put text on a table by selecting an individual cell.
Just click the cell to highlight it and then use your keyboard to enter the text you
want (see Figure 3.5).

FIGURE 3.5

You can select a
desired cell and
type your text.

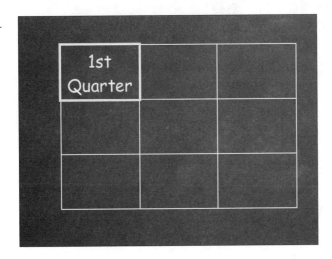

As with any other text, you can change the font, color, and style of table text. By default, the text you type in a table adheres to the text style used in the template you have selected. But that text might not work as well in a table as it does in other cases, so you might have to change it.

To change your text, do the following:

1. Click inside the cell that contains the text you want to change and then drag over the text, holding down the mouse to select it.

2. Select **Format**, **Font**, **Show Fonts** to open the standard Fonts dialog box, where you can select a font family, a typeface, and a size.

3. Use the **Action** drop-down menu in the Fonts dialog box to make any desired font changes. See Chapter 2, "Working with Text," for additional details about the Action drop-down menu.

Of course, you need to use some common sense when you are working with fonts and tables. You want the information to be very clear and quickly readable. For example, take a look at Figures 3.6 and 3.7.

FIGURE 3.6

This table uses the Helvetica font and it is easy to read.

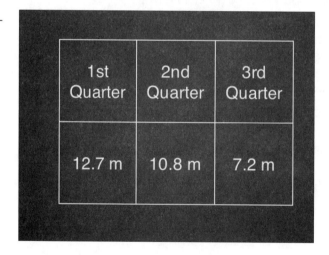

FIGURE 3.7

This table uses the Party LET font. As you can see, it is rather difficult to read.

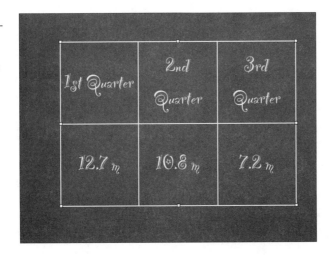

Figures 3.6 and 3.7 use Helvetica, which is a standard Mac font, and Party LET, which is the font most often used for fun text. Obviously, Helvetica is much easier to read, and that's what you want. Table data is not the place to get creative with font styles. As you create tables and enter text, keep the following points in mind:

- **Use clear, easy-to-read fonts, colors, and styles**—If you are going to err, err on the side of plainness. You want the table easy to read (and quick to read as well). Audience members should not have to work to read the table text.

- **Keep it very short**—A couple words in a cell is best. Table text is not the place to wax poetic, so keep it extremely short and informative.

- **Don't overcrowd tables with cells and text**—Remember that a table should show relationships between pieces of information, but your audience should not have to study your table in order to comprehend your intended meaning.

Aligning Text

You can easily manage the alignment of text by using the Table Inspector. Here's how:

1. Click the **Inspector** button on the toolbar or select **View**, **Show Inspector**. The Table Inspector appears.

2. Click the **Table** button on the Table Inspector.

3. As shown in Figure 3.8, you have the option to manage the alignment of the text within your table. The first four buttons allow you to left-justify, center, right-justify, or simply justify, which distributes text evenly. Select a cell that contains text and click the alignment option you want. Keep in mind that center alignment (which is the default) often looks the best.

FIGURE 3.8

Use the Alignment buttons to determine how text aligns within a cell.

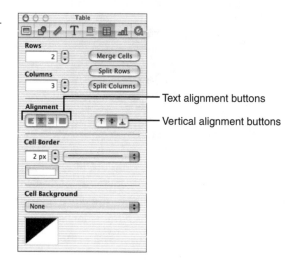

Text alignment buttons

Vertical alignment buttons

4. To manage the vertical alignment of text within the cell, use the vertical alignment buttons on the Text Inspector to align text to the top of the cell, the center of the cell, or the bottom of the cell. Again, the center option is the default and most often looks the best. Figure 3.9 shows three columns. The first column has the text aligned to the top of the cell, the middle column has the text aligned to the center of the cell, and the last column has the text aligned to the bottom of the cell.

As with other things in Keynote, you can return to these options and change them at any time.

FIGURE 3.9

The alignment options give you control over the appearance of a table.

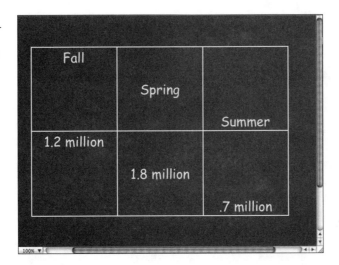

Quick Text Tricks

Before we move on, there are a couple quick text options I want to mention that will make your work easier. First, keep in mind that you can work with individual cells of text, multiple selected cells, or an entire table. To make a change, such as a font or alignment change, to the text within a certain cell, just select the cell. If you want to change several cells at the same time, hold down the ⌘ key on your keyboard and select the cells. You can then change the font or alignment of these cells all at the same time. Finally, you do the same thing by simply selecting the entire table. Just click outside the table to make sure none of the cells are selected and then click the table one time to select it. You can then use the Fonts dialog box to change all the fonts, or you can use the Text Inspector to change the alignment of all the text.

One final tip I would like to point out concerns dragging text. Let's say you are creating a table that has the same text in several cells, which is common in the case of numeric values. In this case, you can simply copy and paste text between cells. Using the mouse, you simply select the desired values and choose **Edit**, **Copy**. Then you position the cursor where you want to paste the text or numbers and choose **Edit**, **Paste**.

If you type text in a cell and then decide that you want to move the text, you can simply drag the text to the desired cell and drop it there, as shown Figure 3.10. Just select the cell and drag the text from the selected cell to the new cell where you want the text to reside.

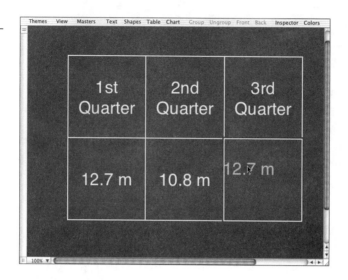

Formatting Cells, Rows, and Columns

You can use the Table Inspector to quickly create simple tables that contain the number of rows and columns you need. You can also use the Table Inspector to create more advanced tables that take advantage of splitting and merging cells so that the table meets your needs.

To adjust cells as needed, you once again use the Table Inspector. Just click the **Inspector** button on the toolbar and then choose the **Table** option at the top of the Inspector.

Choosing the Number of Columns and Rows in a Table

In the first part of the Table Inspector, you can choose the number of rows and columns that you might want, as shown in Figure 3.11. Just click the spinner arrows next to the Rows and Columns fields to increase or decrease the number of rows and columns in the table. The table will automatically adjust to accommodate your change.

caution

You can make tables that are as complex as you want. However, keep in mind that your audience has to be able to interpret your tables. When your audience members look at a table, it should make perfect sense quickly and easily. A table that has a conglomeration of complicated cells often is not readily clear and requires a bit of study. So, once again, err on the side of simplicity and make sure that each table is easy to understand.

FIGURE 3.11

You can easily adjust the number of rows and columns in a table by using the Table Inspector.

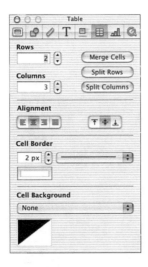

Merging and Splitting Rows and Columns

You can use the Table Inspector to merge cells, split rows, and split columns. First of all, you might not like the default cell construction Keynote gives you, or you might need larger cells than normal. No problem. By using the Table Inspector, you can merge cells together so that they become one. Here's how:

> **tip**
>
> Of course, you can quickly run out of table room on a slide, so you'll have to hone your table down a bit if it is getting too large or consider subdividing the presentation information into two tables on different Keynote slides.

1. Select two or more adjacent cells by holding down the Shift key on your keyboard and clicking the cells (see Figure 3.12).

2. Click the **Merge Cells** button in the Table Inspector to merge the cells together (see Figure 3.13).

Just as you can merge rows or columns, you can also split them. You might use this feature when you need to subdivide data so that it is easier to read. Follow these steps:

1. To split a row, column, or cell, select it with your mouse. If you need to select multiple cells, hold down the Shift key and click them.

2. On the Table Inspector, click either the **Split Rows** button or the**Split Columns** button, as needed. Essentially, the Split Rows button creates a horizontal split in the cell, and the Split Columns button creates a vertical split.

FIGURE 3.12
You hold down
the Shift key to
select multiple
cells.

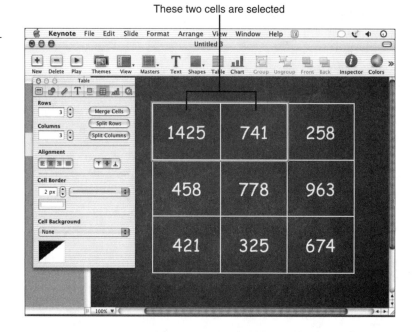

FIGURE 3.13
Two cells
become one.

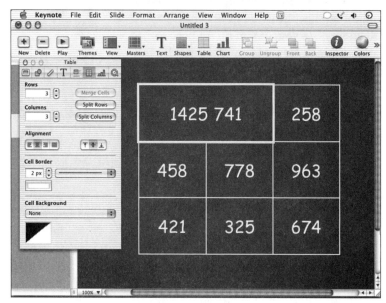

Adjusting the Cell Border

You can easily change the borders of individual cells or of a whole table by using the Cell Border section of the Table Inspector. To change the thickness of a table or cell border, follow these steps:

1. Click the table once to select the whole table or click the individual cell whose border you want to adjust.

2. Click the **Inspector** button on the toolbar and then click the **Table** button at the top of the Inspector.

3. Click the up and down spinner arrows next to the **Cell Border** field to increase or decrease the thickness of the border. Alternatively, you can click the pop-up menu next to the Cell Border field and choose a line thickness from the list. Your changes are automatically applied to the table so you can see the effect right away.

4. If you don't like the look, just make additional changes on the Table Inspector, or you can select **Edit**, **Undo** to undo your changes.

Adjusting borders has a few helpful uses, such as

- You can easily change the overall look of a table by simply adjusting all the cell borders and colors. As you can see in Figure 3.14, just a slight increase in cell border thickness can make the table look a bit stronger.

FIGURE 3.14
A stronger cell border can make a table stand out.

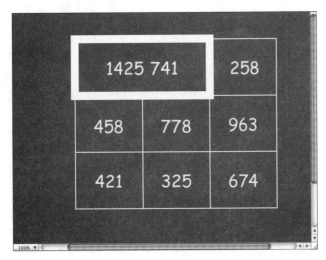

- You can call attention to individual cells by making a cell's border a bit stronger than the borders of other cells. This works well when you use additional styles with your text, such as boldface, as you can see in Figure 3.15.

FIGURE 3.15

You can make individual cells stand out by adjusting their borders.

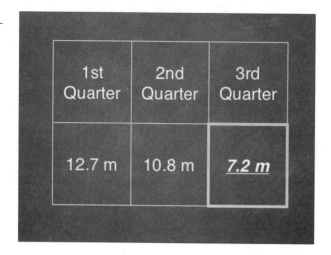

You can also change the color of a cell or table border:

1. Click the table once to select the whole table or click the individual cell whose border you want to adjust.

2. Click the **Inspector** button on the toolbar and then click the **Table** button at the top of the Inspector.

3. Click the color box just below the **Cell Border** field in the Table Inspector. The Colors dialog box opens, as shown in Figure 3.16.

4. Use the option buttons across the top of the Colors dialog box to select a method of picking a color. For example, Figure 3.16 uses a spectrum to find a new color. Simply locate the color you want and click it to apply it to your table.

5. You can adjust the opacity of the table border color by using the **Opacity** slider. When set to a lower number, the Opacity setting allows some of the background color to bleed through the border color, giving it a somewhat transparent look. You can set it to a higher number to achieve a more solid-colored border.

tip

If you start to change a cell border, ask yourself why you're doing it. There is a danger with any software to do things simply because you can rather than for any particular need. Always take a step back and look critically at your table to make sure you have a good reason for the change you are making.

FIGURE 3.16
This is the standard Mac OS X Colors dialog box that you see any time you start to change the color of anything in Keynote.

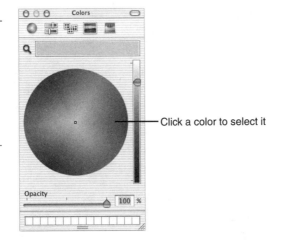

Click a color to select it

6. Click the **Close** button in the upper-left corner of the Colors dialog box when you are finished.

Again, feel free to customize the color in any way you like, but make sure the color you choose matches the rest of your slide colors and simply looks good. Remember: You want the data in the table, not the table border, to get the attention.

Choosing the Cell Background

You are not stuck with the default theme background coming through your table. If you like, and if your slide looks good with the option, you can fill the table background by using the Cell Background feature, which is also found in the Table Inspector. This option works great because it can make your table stand out a bit and you can use contrasting colors against other slide elements. You can even use an image to fill the background if you like. For example, in Figure 3.17, I have used the Table Inspector to add an image fill, and I have scaled the image to fill the entire table, simply by clicking a few drop-down menu options. It's that easy!

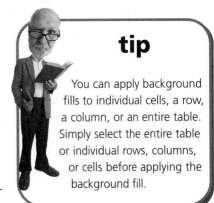

tip

You can apply background fills to individual cells, a row, a column, or an entire table. Simply select the entire table or individual rows, columns, or cells before applying the background fill.

FIGURE 3.17
Image Fill is just
one of the cell
background
options.

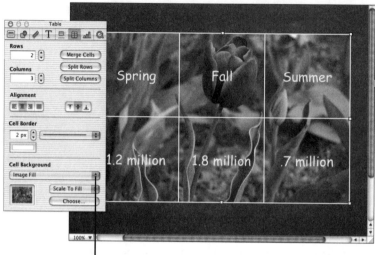

Fill drop-down menu

Interested? I thought so! Here's how you do it:

1. Select the table.

2. Click the **Inspector** button on the toolbar and then click the **Table Inspector** option.

3. On the Table Inspector, click the **Cell Background** drop-down menu and choose an option. You can apply a color fill, a gradient fill (which uses two contrasting colors that blend into each other), or an image fill. Depending on the option you selected, additional selection options appear under on the Table Inspector so that you can select your color, gradient, or image.

4. Make a selection from the options that appear under on the Table Inspector, and it will be applied to your table.

note

Always take a critical look at your table and make sure the colors, gradients, or images actually look good and match the rest of your slide. And always, remember that these items should help your table content—not detract from it.

Inserting Graphics in Tables

Certainly, text works great in tables, but what if you want to put an image or a picture in one of the cells within a table? For example, let's say that you have some sales numbers, and for a quarter of the year that is not finished, you want to place an image that shows the prospective outcome rather than a number guess. No matter what you want to do, you can put pictures and images in table cells, and Keynote does all the scaling and formatting for you, which is really nice.

To put a graphic in a table, you need to return to the Table Inspector. Select the cell in question on your table, and then under Cell Background on the Table Inspector, drag the image to the image well, or just click **Choose** to locate the image on your Mac.

Choose the **Scale to Fill** option, and the image is scaled to fit inside the cell, as you can see in Figure 3.18. It's simple and easy! At this point, the image is a part of your table, and if you move the table around, the image will stay in the cell and remain formatted correctly.

FIGURE 3.18
You can fill a single cell with an image quickly and easily.

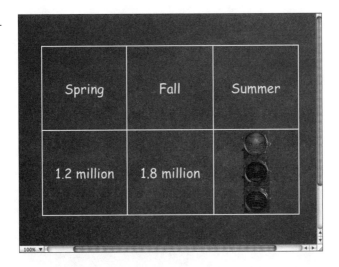

THE ABSOLUTE MINIMUM

Tables are really easy to create and use because Keynote makes them that way. When you work with tables, keep the following issues in mind:

- Think carefully about table content. Use tables to present contrasting information and data that can be viewed in a visual way. Tables work great for series of numbers and information that functions on a timetable basis.

- Enter table text and content just as you would with any other slide element. Use the Fonts dialog box to make adjustments to fonts and text colors as needed.

- Use the Table Inspector to adjust the rows and columns of a table. You can also use the Table Inspector to manage text alignment, cell borders, and cell backgrounds, including background formatting for the entire table.

IN THIS CHAPTER

- Create effective presentation charts
- Make chart data look great
- Choose and work with different chart types
- Use and master chart components to give a presentation an extra edge

4

USING CHARTS

A *chart* is a graphical representation of some information, usually numbers, percentages, and other basic types of data. In a nutshell, a chart is used to make data easier to understand. A chart is a lot like a table in that it presents data in a logical manner. Unlike a table, a chart is a visual representation of data.

In this chapter, you'll learn just about everything there is to know about creating and using charts in Keynote, and you'll see just how easily and beautifully Keynote handles charts.

The Wonderful World of Charts

As you work with Keynote, you'll probably find many opportunities to create charts, depending on the kind of presentations you do. Sales figures, quarterly earnings, growth plans, income and expense, and other types of comparative data are great chart fodder. The good news is that Keynote makes charting rather easy, but Keynote offers a number of formatting and usage options that you need to know about in order to make the most of charts in Keynote.

Chapter 3, "Using Tables," mentions that tables are helpful in a variety of situations, although they're not the most exciting part of creating Keynote presentations. Charts are a different story. Charts give you a great way to make data visual, and the great news about visual data is that it is easier for audience members to understand and retain. In short, a chart gives you a way to make otherwise static data come to life, and that's always a great thing in a presentation. For example, take a look at the chart in Figure 4.1.

FIGURE 4.1

Tables make static data visual.

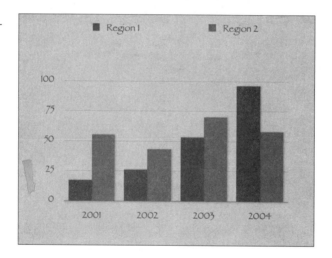

As you can see, this chart makes data interesting. Without the chart, as the speaker, I have to say some things like, "In 2001, Region 1 saw growth of 25,000 while Region 2 saw growth over 50,000, and in 2002...blah, blah, blah." Spoken data like this can lull you into a coma. That's where the beauty of charts comes into play. If I use a Keynote chart, I can easily display the data in a chart format and then talk about the chart content in a much more dynamic way.

When should you use a chart? Here are some quick tips to remember:

■ **Use a chart to represent income and expense figures**—These figures take on extra meaning in a chart format.

■ **Use a chart to show data over a period of time, such as income, growth, and so forth**—You can use the graphical nature of a chart to display the time factor and how the data fits into that time frame.

■ **Use a chart to show relationships between data**—In this case, a typical pie chart can do wonders.

As with any other Keynote element, charts should be clear, concise, and easily understandable. Avoid overly complex charts that are difficult to understand.

Creating a Chart

Like most things in Keynote, an initial chart is quite easy to create. Keynote creates a default chart and plugs in some sample data for you, so with just a couple mouse clicks, you actually have a real chart. Of course, you'll need to customize the chart to meet your needs and so that it displays your actual data, but we'll get to that in upcoming sections. For now, let's create an initial chart:

1. Start a new presentation or open an existing one. If you are starting a new presentation, choose a theme.

2. To make things easier for now, click the **New** button to create a new slide, and then from the **Masters** drop-down menu, choose the **Blank** slide option, as shown in Figure 4.2. This will keep any other template items from getting in your way until you are familiar with charts.

FIGURE 4.2

You can choose the Blank master.

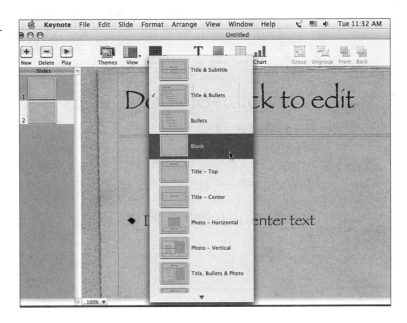

3. Now you are ready to create the chart. Click the **Chart** button on the Keynote toolbar. When you click this button, three things happen automatically, as you can see in Figure 4.3. First, a default chart is created on your slide. Second, the Chart Data Editor appears. Third, the Chart Inspector appears. This is a little overwhelming at first, for certain, but don't worry—you'll learn how to use the Chart Data Editor and the Chart Inspector in upcoming sections.

4. For now, close the Chart Data Editor and the Chart Inspector.

FIGURE 4.3

The chart appears, along with the Chart Data Editor and the Chart Inspector.

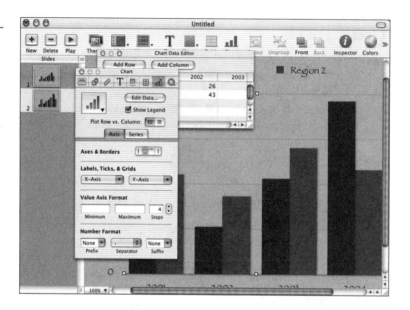

The first thing you might notice is that your chart may take up the entire slide. In fact, you might have to scroll around a bit to even see the entire chart. The good news is that you can resize the chart just as you would any other object, such as a text box, a table, or an image. Just click the chart one time, and the selection handles appear. Then simply drag the selection handles as needed to resize the chart, as shown in Figure 4.4.

tip

If you want to manage the size of a chart at the same time that you create it, just do this: Hold down the **Option** key and click the **Chart** button. Then position your mouse on the slide until it turns into a crosshair. Then simply drag to create a chart of the size you want.

Selection handles

FIGURE 4.4

You can drag the selection handles to resize a chart.

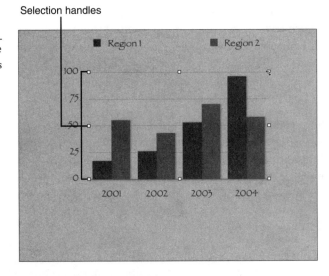

Choosing a Chart Style

After you have created a basic chart, you can use the Chart Inspector to choose a chart style. The different styles available allow you to display your data in a variety of formats. Certain formats are useful for displaying specific kinds of data. For example, parts of a whole work great in a pie chart, and contrasting figures look great in a column chart.

To choose a chart style, you need to open the Chart Inspector. If it is not open already, just click **Inspector** on the toolbar and choose the **Chart** icon on the Inspector.

In the Chart Inspector, you see a chart icon with a drop-down menu. If you click the drop-down menu, you see several different chart style options, as shown in Figure 4.5.

FIGURE 4.5

You click the Chart button to see a chart style selection menu.

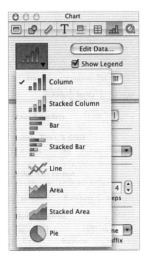

The following sections briefly explain the various chart styles and when you are likely to find each style most helpful. Keep in mind that you have a lot of creative latitude when you choose a chart style, but you can use the following sections as a general guide.

Column Charts

A column chart, which is the default chart Keynote makes for you, presents information in column blocks. The column format uses a different color column for each block of data, and this format works great for showing contrasting data between different items over time. For example, the column format works great if you are showing sales or growths for different regions, stores, products, and so on over a period of time.

Stacked Column Charts

A stacked column chart, as shown in Figure 4.6, can be helpful when you want to show groupings of different data over time. For example, a stacked column chart allows you to use different data items, but they are displayed over time and in a stacked fashion. This kind of chart can be helpful for showing relationships, but it is not very helpful for showing contrasts of data because it tends be confusing to the audience.

FIGURE 4.6

Stacked column charts work well for showing relationships.

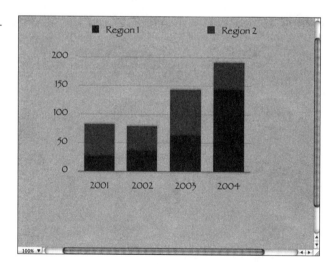

Bar Charts

The bar style essentially does the same thing as a column chart, but it displays the information in a left-to-right bar format, as you can see in Figure 4.7. Therefore, the same kinds of information that work great in a column format also generally work great in a bar format.

FIGURE 4.7

The bar style can be used to show comparisons over time.

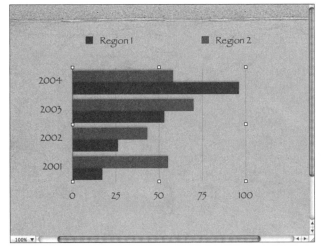

Stacked Bar Charts

The stacked bar chart is the same concept as the stacked column format. Rather than show different regions, it stacks the bars into single bars, noting the differences with different color shading. Once again, this approach can be good for showing relationships or overall progress, but it can be confusing to audience members, so be sure to inspect the choice carefully and ensure that the data is clearly presented.

Line Charts

Line charts, as you can see in Figure 4.8, are great for showing growth or a decline in growth, whether that growth is concerning income, expenses, numbers of people, numbers of departments, or something else. You can use this type of chart to show how several different items compare to each other over time. For example, in Figure 4.8, you can see how Region 1 has grown much more than Region 2 over a period of four years. When you choose a line chart, think in terms of growth because the line feature really helps drive your point home in a graphical way.

note

There is a lot to be said about the aesthetics of a chart. Although bar and column styles can essentially display the same kind of data, one may be better than the other, depending on the data content. For example, a column format may work best when you are talking about revenue because the columns are vertical. We tend think of "rising" or "increasing" revenue, so the vertical columns often look better than horizontal bars would look. However, if you are showing growth or speed, a bar style may work better because we often think of growth or speed in terms of distance, which we conceptualize as horizontal.

FIGURE 4.8

Line charts are great for showing growth over a period of time.

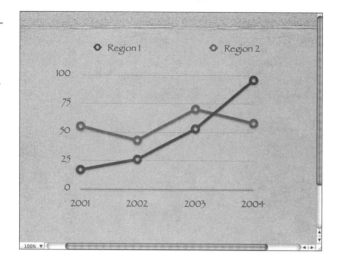

Area Charts

Area charts are similar to line charts in that they can show growth or a decline in growth, but an area chart fills in the area of growth or decline, as you can see in Figure 4.9. The area style often works great when you are trying to dynamically show growth or decline of one or two items, such as the growth of a company or two departments. Be wary of using more than two contrasting items in an area chart because the chart can quickly become confusing to read.

FIGURE 4.9

Area charts can dynamically show growth or decline over a period of time.

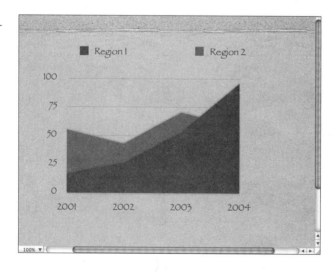

Stacked Area Charts

A stacked area chart works in much the same way as a stacked column chart. Sections of data are stacked in order to show relationships or overall growth. A stacked area chart works well with collections of related data but can be confusing if you are showing contrasting data groups.

Pie Charts

The pie chart, shown in Figure 4.10, is a mainstay of charts and one that you'll use often. Pie charts can show parts of a whole and are especially helpful when you need to break data that belongs to a whole into parts (for example, sales, growth, company divisions). You'll see some additional examples of cool things you can do with pie charts later in this chapter.

FIGURE 4.10

Using a pie chart is a great way to show parts of a whole.

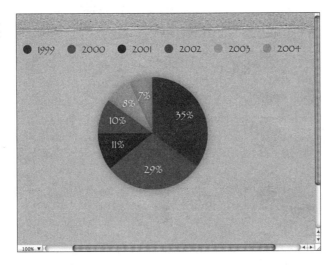

Working with Chart Data

Of course, a chart isn't very helpful unless you can customize the data in it. After all, the purpose of a chart is to show a set of data in a graphical way. So, in order to effectively use charts, you have to manipulate the data so that the chart has real meaning in your presentation. In Keynote, you manage chart data with the Chart Data Editor.

The Chart Data Editor appears automatically when you create a new chart, and if you need to access it after the chart has been created, you can just open the Chart Inspector and click the **Edit Data** button. You can also open it by selecting **Format**, **Chart**, **Show Data Editor**. The Chart Data Editor is shown in Figure 4.11.

FIGURE 4.11

The Chart Data
Editor gives you
an easy way to
input data for
charts.

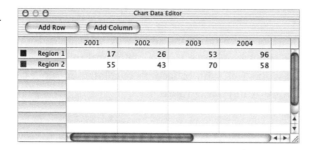

Understanding Chart Data

Before you start editing chart data, it is important that you understand how the
Chart Data Editor handles data. A chart contains two different kinds of data: data
series and data sets. A *data series* is a collection of data taken over time. For example, let's say you are creating a chart that shows income from three different companies over a period of three years. The *data series* is the three companies over three
specific years. In other words, it is a series of data. On the other hand, a *data set* is
the income levels of one of those companies. The set represents income of that particular company. With the other companies and the amount of time, the collection
of sets becomes a series.

Now, you don't have to study the terms *data series* and *data set*; there is no test, of
course, but if you have a firm understanding that charts represent collections of
data sets that make up data series, it will make your work with Keynote much less
confusing.

As you are creating data sets, a single piece of information in a set is called a *data
point*. For example, if a company made 10.3 million dollars in 2002, that is a data
point.

Data points make up data sets, and data sets make up data series. The whole chart,
then, is used to communicate what could be head-spinning information in an easy-
to-understand graphical format.

Using the Chart Data Editor

As you work with the Chart Data Editor, you see that it is essentially a spreadsheet
made up of data series, data sets, and data points. Figure 4.12 shows the Chart Data
Editor again, with some callouts to make things a bit easier.

Data set

FIGURE 4.12

The Chart Data
Editor allows
you to input
series of data
with data sets
and data points.

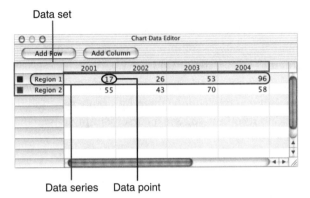

Data series   Data point

So, to get the data you want in your chart, you have to edit the data series values, the data sets, and the individual points of the data sets. The good news is that this is easy because the Chart Data Editor allows you to simply change and enter those values.

Let's walk through an example together, and you'll see how to use the Chart Data Editor. Let's say you are giving a presentation on income for a company. The company has four divisions: North, South, East, and West. You want to create a column graph showing income over the years 2000, 2001, and 2002. Here is how to create the chart:

1. The first thing you want to do in the Chart Data Editor is to make some changes to the overall data series. First, you are going to change the default Region 1 and Region 2 to represent your values, which are North, South, East, and West. To change the value, just click the cell to highlight it and then double-click so that a cursor appears.

2. Press the Delete key to remove the default label and then retype your own. Repeat this process as needed. Figure 4.13 shows the values to North, South, East, and West being changed.

Retype data values

FIGURE 4.13

Click a cell to
select it and
then retype the
desired label.

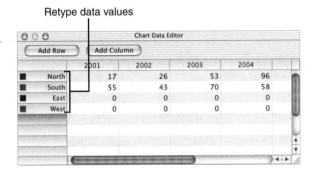

Notice that when you add a new cell value, a color box is automatically added. These colors are used to distinguish the different data in your chart. For example, if you use a column format, then each column of data will have a different color (refer to Figure 4.13).

3. Change the year values. The default chart already has some time values plugged in, but you can change them by simply selecting the cell and then double-clicking it so that you see a cursor. Simply retype the value you want (see Figure 4.14).

Data cells
Chart Data Editor
Add Row
Add Column
2000
2001
2002
2004
North
17
26
53
96
South
55
43
70
58
East
0
0
0
0
West
0
0
0
0

FIGURE 4.14
You click the cell to select it and then retype the desired value.

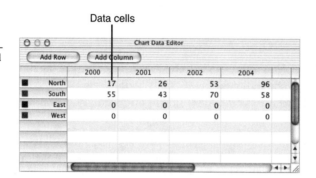

4. Notice that you have a leftover column from the default chart. This is no problem. You can delete any column by simply clicking the column heading one time. This selects the column, as you can see in Figure 4.15. Then you just press the Delete key to remove it.

Chart Data Editor
Add Row
Add Column
2000
2001
2002
2004
North
17
26
53
96
South
55
43
70
58
East
0
0
0
0
West
0
0
0
0

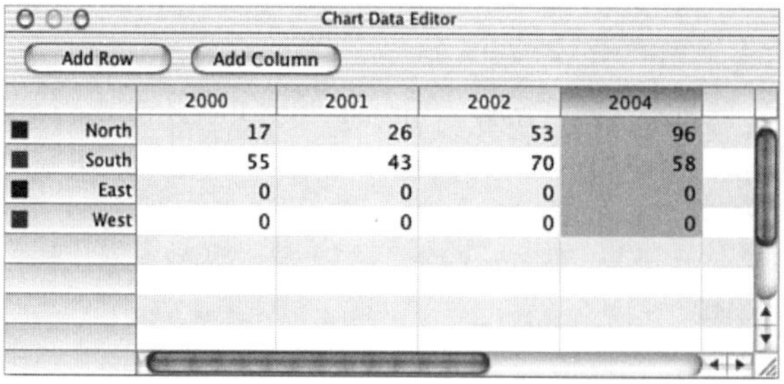

FIGURE 4.15
You click a column to select it and then press the Delete key.

5. Enter the desired data points. In this case, you are entering sales figures for each region for the three years. Just click inside a cell and type your new data.

Figure 4.16 shows the completed changes in the Chart Data Editor, and Figure 4.17 shows the changes applied to the chart. You have easily and quickly created a chart that displays the income data over the years 2000–2002 for each of the regions. That's all there is to it!

FIGURE 4.16
The Chart Data Editor now has the complete data.

		2000	2001	2002		
■	North	10.3	7.2	9.7		
■	South	4.3	2.6	3.8		
■	East	6.8	5.4	3.2		
■	West	12.4	13.2	11.9		

FIGURE 4.17
The new chart is automatically displayed.

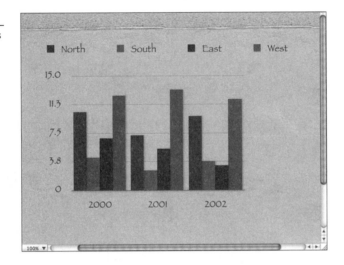

Of course, you might need to add rows or columns, and that's no problem. Just use the Add Row and Add Col umn buttons in the Chart Data Editor as needed to increase the number of rows and columns in the chart.

Using the Chart Inspector

You need to consider two more items concerning chart data. These items are found on the Chart Inspector instead of the Chart Data Editor, which may cause you some confusion at first.

The Chart Inspector, shown in Figure 4.18, has a Show legend check box and a Plot Row vs. Column button option directly below the Edit Data button. Here's what you can do with these:

caution

Charts need to be somewhat simple. Excess rows and columns become difficult to understand, so always try to stay on the side of simplicity. Using two slides with two different charts to convey data is much better than using one slide with a very complicated chart. Keep your message clear and simple!

FIGURE 4.18

The Chart
Inspector has a
Show legend
check box.

- **Show Legend**—When this option is unchecked, the legend is removed from the slide. For example, in Figure 4.17, you see the North, South, East, and West labels and the color legend at the top of the slide. Clearing the Show legend check box would remove these from the slide. Doing this might help clean up your slide a bit. A chart can be difficult to understand without a legend, though, so think carefully before you remove it. If you are providing handouts to your audience members, they may be able to understand the chart when referring to it at a later time, so unless you have a specific reason for doing so, keep the legend on the chart.

- **Plot Row vs. Column**—This option transposes the basic flow of the chart. For example, in Figure 4.17, the data series is represented by the rows in the Chart Data Editor. If you transpose the row and column, the data set is represented by the row instead of the column, as you can see in Figure 4.19. Naturally, this causes the chart not to make any sense because I wrote the data series information into the Chart Data Editor using rows. However, the point is that you can use rows or columns of data in the Chart Data Editor if you like. Simply use the Plot Row vs. Column selection buttons on the Chart Inspector to transpose the data.

FIGURE 4.19
The data is
transposed when
you use the Plot
Row vs. Column
feature on the
Chart Inspector.

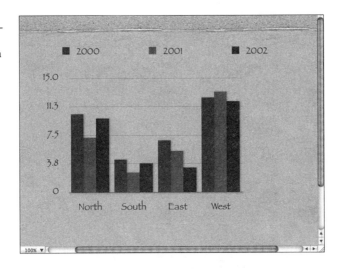

Formatting Charts

The elements, or different parts of a chart, can be formatted in basically any way so that your chart looks exactly the way you want it to. The following sections describe what you can do.

Moving the Chart Legend

As you have learned in this chapter, a chart can use a legend or not—the decision is up to you. By using the Chart Inspector, you can remove the legend or leave it on a slide (as it is by default). However, what if you don't like the location of the legend? By default, the legend appears at the top of the chart, but the legend is actually a separate text box that you can move around, enlarge, reduce, and change as you like.

You can move the legend around, and you can even reformat the fonts and colors. You can also move a legend to a different slide. However, there is a caveat you need to keep in mind: The legend is tied to the chart, even though it is an individual piece that can be moved around. When you change or update a chart, the legend is changed or updated as well. However, if you move the legend to a different slide, it becomes disconnected from the chart and will not be updated if you make any changes to your chart. Just keep this point in mind.

tip

As a general rule, it is not a good idea to move the legend to a different slide because the legend helps audience members understand the chart.

To customize the legend, you just click it on the slide, and the familiar text box and selection handles appear. At this point, you can simply drag the legend to a new location (such as the bottom of the chart), and you can also use the selection handles to resize the legend if you like. As you can see in Figure 4.20, I have moved the legend to the side of the chart and resized it so that the legend items appear in a vertical fashion. This frees up more room at the top of the chart, where I can insert a title, a picture, or anything else I might want.

FIGURE 4.20

You can click the legend to see the text box and selection handles, and then you can then move it around or resize it as you like.

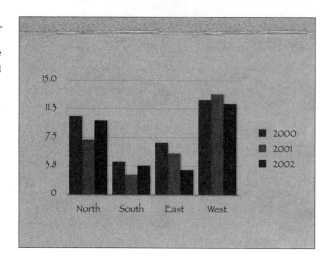

Changing Chart Colors

You can change the colors of bars, edges, and area shapes that appear on a chart, just as you can change the colors of any other object on a slide. You can change the colors, apply shading, fill with an image, adjust opacity, and do other tasks by using the Graphic Inspector. You'll learn more about the Graphic Inspector in Chapter 5, "Working with Graphics," but for now, here's a quick sample to pique your curiosity:

1. On your slide, select one of the chart elements, such as a column. When you do so, all columns in the series become selected, and you see the selection handles marking your selection, as shown in Figure 4.21.

2. Open the Inspector by clicking the **Inspector** icon on the toolbar and then click the **Graphic** button at the top of the Inspector. Using the Graphic Inspector, as shown in Figure 4.22, you can change any of the color qualities of your selection. (See Chapter 5 to learn more about the features of the Graphic Inspector.)

FIGURE 4.21
Selection han-
dles appear
when an ele-
ment is selected
on a chart.

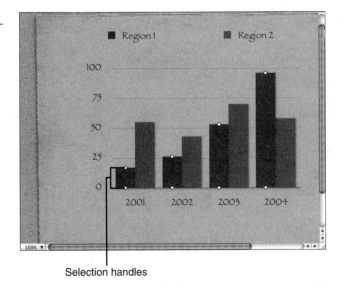

Selection handles

FIGURE 4.22
You can use the
Graphic
Inspector to
change objects.

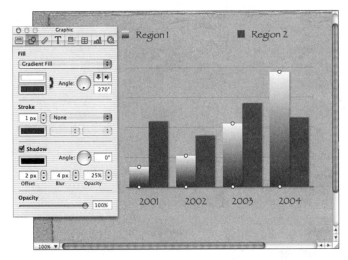

Changing Chart Fonts

Just as you can change fonts and the color of text in a text box, you can also change them on a chart by simply selecting them and opening the Font dialog box. Just select **Format**, **Font**, **Show Fonts**. On the Font dialog box, choose a font family, a typeface (if necessary), and the desired font size. Use the **Text** button options on the Font dialog box to make style and color changes. (See Chapter 2, "Working with Text," for more details.) Note that if you select text that is tied to a data point or an axis label (which we'll talk about in the next section), all the text for that data is also selected.

Working with Labels and Axis Markings

In charts, axis markings basically determine the values that are displayed on the vertical axis (that is, the y-axis) from which you read the data point values. For example, if your data sets reflect income from 5 million to 25 million, the vertical axis reflects those values so you can understand what the columns or bars mean. For vertical charts, the y-axis shows the values (for example, the years in the previous examples).

You don't have to worry about all those definitions, but you should know that you can do a lot of customization work with the flow of the axis markings and their labels by using the Chart Inspector.

Select your chart on the slide and then open the Chart Inspector. Click the Axis tab, and you can see the axis options and features that you can customize according to your needs, as shown in Figure 4.23. The following sections describe what you can do.

FIGURE 4.23

You can use the Axis feature on the Chart Inspector to customize a chart.

Axes & Borders

The Axes & Borders portion of the Axis tab simply allows you to decide what borders you want to use around the axis and general border of a chart. Just click the button options to use them—that's all you have to do. Figure 4.24 shows a chart with no borders enabled, and Figure 4.25 shows a chart with all borders enabled.

FIGURE 4.24

This chart does not use any borders.

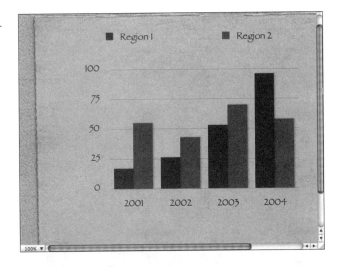

FIGURE 4.25

This chart uses borders on all sides.

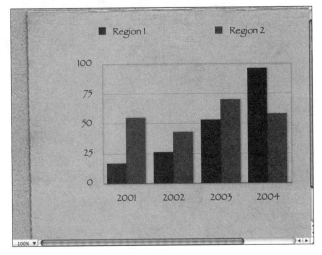

Labels, Ticks, & Grids

The Labels, Ticks, & Grids portion of the Axis tab enables you to control how labels, ticks, and grids are used on the x-axis and y-axis. If you click either the X-Axis or Y-Axis drop-down menu, you'll see a number of options that allow you to customize the labels, ticks, and grids in the chart. These options are self-explanatory, but you should spend some time playing with the options so you can see the many different ways a chart can appear.

Value Axis Format

The Value Axis Format portion of the Axis tab allows you to control what you see on the value axis. For example, Figure 4.25 shows that the value axis on the chart has range of 0 to 100. You can easily change the values by entering new minimum and maximum values in the Minimum, Maximum, and Steps boxes under Value Axis Format. You can also change the number of steps on the chart. This feature allows you to adjust the value axis so that it is easier to read and understand. For example, Figure 4.26 shows Minimum being set to 100, Maximum being set to 500, and Steps being increased from 5 (refer to Figure 4.25) to 8. The results are made automatically in the chart.

FIGURE 4.26

You can change the value axis as needed. The results of the change appear on the chart.

Change the value axis here

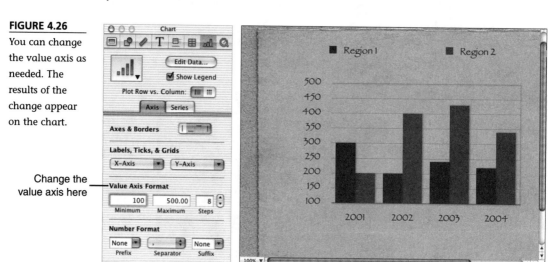

Number Format

The Number Format portion of the Axis tab gives you more customization options for the numbers on the value axis. It enables you to add prefixes, separators, and suffixes to the value axis. For example, if you are using value axis values such as 100, 200, 300, and so forth, you can use the Prefix drop-down menu to add a prefix so that they read $100, $200, $300, and so forth.

Formatting Data Series Elements

The Chart Inspector has a Series tab that provides some helpful and easy options for formatting data series elements. Note that some series options apply to certain kinds of charts, so not all options are enabled for each kind of chart, as you can see in Figure 4.27.

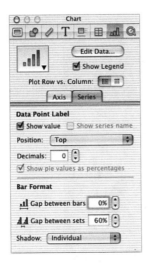

The data series options, described in the following list,
are really easy to use:

Remember to select
your chart before (or after)
opening the Chart Inspector so
that the options are active.

- **Data Point Label**—These options enable
  you to choose to show values on the data
  points. This basically puts the actual value
  on the column or bar, as you can see in
  Figure 4.28. If series are named, you can
  show that option, too, by checking the
  "Show series name" check box. You can use
  the Position drop-down menu to decide
  where you want the labels to be placed,
  such as on the top, bottom, and so forth.
  You can also add decimals if needed by typing the appropriate value in the Decimals
  text box or using the spinner arrows to choose a value. If you are using a
  pie chart, you can choose to select the "Show pie values as percentages"
  check box.

- **Bar Format**—This section of the Series axis enables you to put spaces
  between bars and sets of bars. It also enables you to adjust the shadowing
  used on the bars by using the Shadow drop-down menu. You just change the
  percentage values in the text boxes in this section to make adjustments for
  the visual appeal you want.

Data point labels

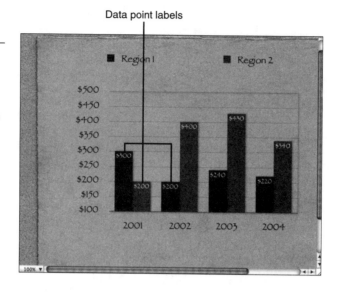

FIGURE 4.28

The Data Point Label section of the Series tab makes the actual data into labels on columns, bars, and pie charts.

Special Issues with Pie Charts

For the most part, all charts work basically the same. However, there are some special issues and features with pie charts that I want to point out. First, you use the Chart Data Editor to enter values for a pie chart, just as you do with any other chart. However, due to the nature of the pie chart, only the first row of a data series is used in the pie chart. Whereas multiple rows work great with bar charts, a pie chart simply cannot display data this way. However, you can choose to chart any data set by simply moving it to the first row in the Chart Data Editor.

In addition, keep in mind that you can use the Data Point Label section on the Series tab in the Chart Inspector to change the basic appearance of the data point labels, and you can format colors of each piece of the pie chart by using the Graphic Inspector, just as you can with any other element on a chart. You can also learn more about the Graphic Inspector in Chapter 5.

One cool feature of the pie chart is that you can detach pieces of the pie for emphasis. To do so, just follow these steps:

1. Select the chart and then click the desired pie wedge to select it. If you want to select additional wedges, just hold down the ⌘ key and click them as well.

tip

You can change the opacity and shadowing feature by using the Graphic Inspector. See Chapter 5 to learn more. Also, how would you like for individual pie wedges to fly on to the slide and build the pie before your audience's eyes? You can do this by using builds, which you'll learn more about in Chapter 8, "Exploring Transitions and Builds."

2. Open the **Inspector** and then click the **Chart** button at the top of the Inspector.

3. On the Series tab, choose **Individual** from the **Shadow** menu.

4. Use the **Explode Wedge** slider bar to move the wedge away from the pie, as shown in Figure 4.29.

FIGURE 4.29

You can move the Explode Wedge slider bar to move the wedge away from the rest of the pie.

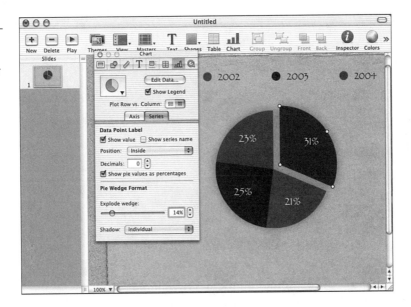

THE ABSOLUTE MINIMUM

Charts are really easy to create and use, and they are very versatile in Keynote. When you work with charts, keep the following issues in mind:

- Use the Chart button on the toolbar to quickly create a chart.
- The Chart Inspector allows you to choose a chart style and to use the Axis and Series tabs to format basically all portions of a chart.
- Enter and manipulate chart data as needed by using the Chart Data Editor.

5

WORKING WITH GRAPHICS

A key concept in education circles is that people learn in different ways. Now, that probably didn't rock your world. You don't have to have a Ph.D. in education to know that different people learn in different ways. Some of us learn most easily by seeing, some learn most easily by hearing, and some people learn best by doing. You probably gravitate more to one of those categories than to the others, and the important point here is simply that your audience members are the same.

Because many people learn best by sight, graphics are a very important part of a presentation and a very important part of using Keynote. In this chapter, you'll learn how to use graphics in Keynote and how to make the most of them in your presentations.

Understanding How to Use Graphics in Presentations

Because visual learning is very helpful (and often necessary) for many people, Keynote slides are more than simply a "help." They are a major learning tool, and one of the main ways you can help your audience members learn is to use graphics on your Keynote slides. Graphics include such items as drawings, line art, photos, clip art, and basically anything else that can be looked at.

No, I'm not going to jump off into communication theory. However, if you'll stick with me for the next page or so, you'll learn some important ideas about using graphics that will make your work with Keynote more productive and make you a better presenter. In the end, you'll be able to better use graphics to communicate your message to the audience.

Graphics are really designed to help people understand something visually. Drawings can help people understand a concept, clip art can replace text and communicate meaning, and you can use a photo to show people something much better than you could by talking about it. Although it's true that a picture is worth a thousand words, it takes the right use of a picture or graphic to communicate what you want your audience to know.

Using Graphics to Make Text Easier to Understand

Graphics can be used to make text easier to understand. This is an important point and a proper use of graphics. The easiest way to make my point here is to show you an example (hey, I'm using a graphic to make my point!). Just take a look at the examples shown in Figure 5.1.

What is the difference between the examples in Figure 5.1? The image on the left presents basic text information on a slide. The information is accurate, but look at the image on the right. With just the simple use of some graphic shapes, the text is broken into a flowchart format that is easier to read, easier to understand, and, most importantly, easier to remember.

This is a major point concerning graphics: Graphics can use basic text to show a flow of information or a flow of thought. Your audience members are more likely to remember instructions and details that are organized in a graphical way. Basically, you are creating a mental picture with the information, and most people remember pictures more easily than simple text information. This is one way that graphics can greatly help communicate your message.

FIGURE 5.1

Images can help
relate the mes-
sage of your text.

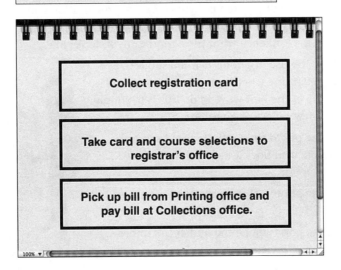

Using Graphic Shapes to Enhance Presentations

A second way that graphics can help communicate text-based information is through what I like to call "helping graphics." Helping graphics do not directly provide information, but they give emphasis to other information you want your audience members to keep in mind. This is one place where clip art and graphic symbols can be really helpful. They dress up your slides, call attention to certain details or blocks of information, and help your audience members more easily remember that information. For example, take a look at the simple slide in Figure 5.2.

FIGURE 5.2

The graphic in
this slide calls
attention to a
detail.

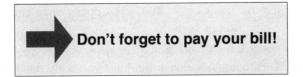

As you can see, the arrow graphic doesn't really communicate anything in and of itself, but it calls attention to the text at hand. By using a graphic, you can call out specific information and help audience members keep in mind the importance of the information.

Using Photos in Presentations

Another use of graphics concerns photos. The good news is that Keynote is rather flexible concerning photos, and you can import photos directly into Keynote and work with them in several ways, which you will explore later in this chapter.

The first thing to address when it comes to photos is when you should use them. In many cases, the use of a photo is dictated by the presentation content. If you are talking about the Grand Canyon, you really need to include at least a few slides that actually show the audience what the Grand Canyon looks like.

In other cases, the use of photos is more subjective. You need to determine whether a photo is really necessary, and one of the best ways to do this is to simply ask yourself a few reflective questions:

- Does the photo truly reflect what I am talking about and does it help the flow of my presentation?
- Does the photo help communicate my message?
- Does the photo make the audience's understanding of my content easier?

If you can answer "yes" to one of these, then you should probably use the photo. If not, you should carefully consider whether the photo is really helpful.

Any photo you use in a Keynote presentation needs to be of high quality. If the photo is not of high quality and it is difficult to view, consider skipping it.

Working with the Colors Dialog Box

Before you can get into the intricacies of adding and editing graphics on a slide, you should be aware of all the options you have for working with color in Keynote. Keep in mind that some of this information will apply to things other than graphics (like text or borders) because the same Colors dialog box opens when you need to choose a color for just about anything in Keynote.

As you might have noticed, the Colors dialog box gives you several options for picking a color. If the Colors dialog box has intimidated you a bit, don't worry. You've come to the right place. There are five button options you can use on the Colors dialog box, and the following sections show you how to use them.

Color Wheel

The Color Wheel option, shown in Figure 5.3, allows you to choose a color from a spectrum of colors presented in a wheel. Just move the slider bar to the right of the dialog box to find the right color hue and then click your mouse on the color you want within the wheel. The color you select is displayed in the color box at the top of the dialog box. Just by clicking around in the wheel and moving the slider bar as needed, you can locate a very fine color selection.

FIGURE 5.3

The Color Wheel option gives you an easy way to pick a color.

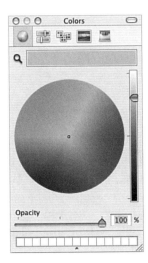

Color Sliders

The Color Sliders option allows you to choose from some different sets of color slides, giving you a fine level of control over the color you want to use. If you click the drop-down menu, you can choose Gray Scale Slider, RGB (Red, Green, Blue) Sliders, CMYK (Cyan, Magenta, Yellow, and Black) Sliders, or HSB (Hue, Saturation, and Brightness) Sliders. If you aren't familiar with these, stick with RGB for anything that is going to be shown on a monitor or projector. On the other hand, CMYK colors work great for printed slides.

After you choose a category that most fits the color you want, simply move the slider bars around to find the exact color (see Figure 5.4). You can also enter percentages instead of using the sliders, but the sliders are easier to use.

FIGURE 5.4

The Color Slider
option allows
you to choose
different slider
options in order
to get the color
you want.

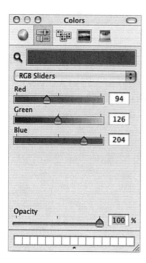

Color Palettes

The Color Palettes option gives you a list of different color options, based on palettes
(see Figure 5.5). Under the List drop-down menu, you can choose Apple colors,
Crayons, or Web Safe Colors, or you can open other color palette options, if you
have any additional palettes installed on your Mac. After you have chosen a palette,
you simply scroll through the list of colors available from that palette and click the
one you want.

FIGURE 5.5

The Color
Palettes option
allows you to
choose colors
from different
palettes.

Image Palettes

The Image Palettes option gives you a basic spectrum of color (see Figure 5.6). You can click within the spectrum to select the actual color that you want to use. This option is very similar to the Color Wheel option.

FIGURE 5.6

The Image Palettes option allows you to choose colors from a spectrum of color.

Crayons

The Crayons option presents you with a collection of digital crayons, and you simply click the crayon color you want to use (see Figure 5.7). The purpose of this option is to give you a collection of standard colors that you can easily click and use.

FIGURE 5.7

You can use the Crayons option to choose basic colors.

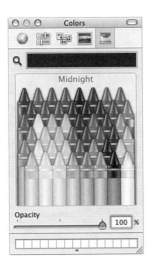

note

Notice that for all options on the Colors dialog box, you can adjust the opacity of the color you choose by moving the Opacity slider bar at the bottom of the Colors dialog box. Once again, the opacity, which adjusts the transparency of a color, gives you more color appearance options.

Working with Line Art

Line art includes basic drawings, such as rectangles, squares, arrows, and so forth. When you're using Keynote, you can simply select one of these items, and it will automatically appear on the slide. From there, you can resize the object and change its overall properties. The following sections explore the options.

Inserting Shapes

When it comes to shapes and objects, Keynote provides you with only a line, a rectangle, an oval, two triangle options, and an arrow—at least from the toolbar. You can add more shapes and objects from the Image Library, which we'll explore later in this chapter.

Of course, you can resize these options to customize them, but these are the only available line art options (see Figure 5.8). Keynote calls these graphics *shapes*.

FIGURE 5.8

Keynote calls the default line art options *shapes*.

To insert a shape onto a slide, do this:

1. Open the slide that you want to add a shape to.

2. Click the **Shapes** button on the toolbar and then click whatever shape you want. The new shape appears on the slide.

After you place the shape on a slide, you are free to manipulate it in any way that you need. For example, you can drag the shape to the correct location on the slide, or you can resize it as needed. If you select the shape, selection handles appear. You can then simply drag the selection handles to resize the shape as needed (see Figure 5.9).

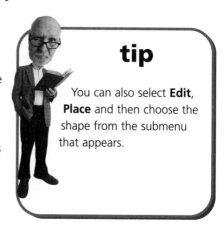

tip

You can also select **Edit**, **Place** and then choose the shape from the submenu that appears.

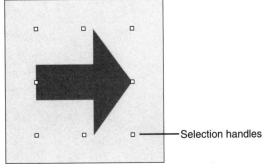

—Selection handles

You can also change the overall look of a shape by clicking and dragging different selection handles located around the shape until the desired shape is achieved. For example, Figure 5.10 shows a couple default arrows after I have changed them by simply moving some of the selection handles. This, of course, gives you a lot of flexibility to make a shape look the way you want.

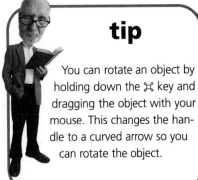

tip

You can rotate an object by holding down the ⌘ key and dragging the object with your mouse. This changes the handle to a curved arrow so you can rotate the object.

FIGURE 5.10
You can change
the look of
default shapes by
dragging the
selection handles.

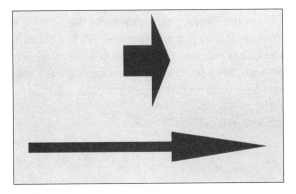

Filling a Shape with Color

When you insert a shape, it uses the current theme's default fill color. That might work just fine for your needs, but you have a lot of different options for fill color.

To manage the fill, you need to open the Graphic Inspector. Click the **Inspector** button on the toolbar, and then choose the **Graphic** button on the Inspector to open the Graphic Inspector (see Figure 5.11).

FIGURE 5.11

You can use the Graphic Inspector to manipulate graphics.

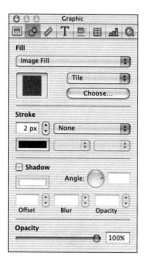

You can fill an image with a color fill, a gradient fill, or an image fill, or you can choose not to use a fill at all by making a selection from the **Fill** drop-down menu in the Graphic Inspector. The Graphic Inspector's other options, described in the following sections, change to reflect the type of fill you have selected.

Color Fill

If you choose Color Fill in the Fill drop-down menu in the Graphic Inspector, a Color box appears just below the Fill drop-down menu (see Figure 5.12). You click the Color box to open the Colors window. From there, you can choose the color you want to fill the object with. Keep in mind that you can click the color wheel option on the Colors dialog box in order to fine-tune your color selection.

Click to open the Colors dialog box

FIGURE 5.12

You can use a color fill option on a shape.

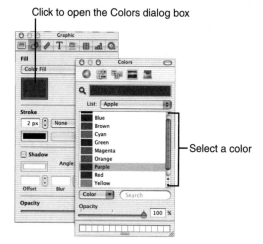

Select a color

Gradient Fill

If you choose Gradient Fill in the Fill drop-down menu in the Graphic Inspector, you have the option to choose the two gradient colors you will use by clicking the color boxes and choosing the colors from the Colors dialog box. A *gradient* is a combination of two colors that fade out across the slide. For example, one part of a slide might be black, which then fades to gray across the slide.

You can then adjust the angle of the gradient by dragging the wheel or using the arrow buttons, as shown in Figure 5.13. These features enable you to completely customize the gradient.

FIGURE 5.13

You can use a gradient fill option in a shape.

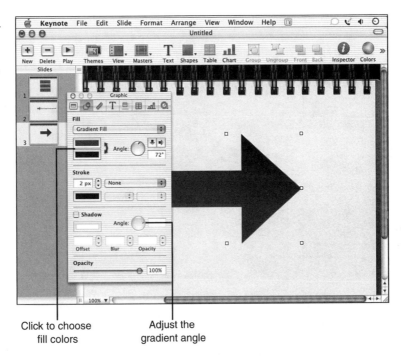

Click to choose fill colors

Adjust the gradient angle

To select and adjust a gradient, follow these steps:

1. Select the object on the slide.

2. Open the **Graphic Inspector** and choose **Gradient Fill** from the **Fill** drop-down menu.

3. Click the color boxes to define the colors that should be used in the gradient. Clicking the color boxes opens the Colors dialog box, where you can select the color you want to use.

4. Adjust the angle of the gradient as desired by sliding the angle wheel. The changes appear on the selected object so that you can find the gradient position you want.

Image Fill

Another really cool thing you can do with a shape is fill it with an image. To do this, you choose the Image Fill option in the Graphic Inspector's Fill drop-down menu and then click the Choose button to select the image you want to fill with. Then you can use the scale drop-down menu to scale the image. The options include scaling so that the image fits within your shape, scales to the fill, stretches to fit, or is left at the original size; you can also tile the image. Figure 5.14 shows an example of an image fill that is scaled to fit the shape. As you might imagine, this feature gives you a lot of different options.

Scaling options

FIGURE 5.14

An image fill can create another layer of interest in a presentation when it is used appropriately.

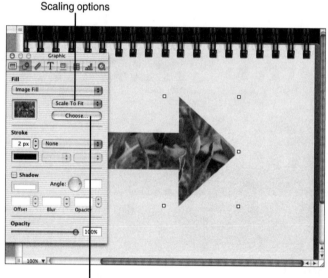

Click to import an image

To use an image fill, follow these steps:

1. Select the object on the slide.

2. Open the **Graphic Inspector** and choose **Image Fill** from the **Fill** drop-down menu.

3. Click the **Choose** button. The Open dialog box appears; in this dialog box, you can locate on your Mac the image you want to use.

4. Locate the image, select it, and click the **Open** button. The Image now appears in the object on your slide.

You can use the drop-down menu to adjust the image as necessary. You can choose to tile the image, stretch it, scale it, or use the original size.

Stroke

The Stroke options in the Graphic Inspector enable you to outline a graphic shape. Essentially, the stroke feature simply makes a graphic look a bit sharper and more defined on the slide. You can choose from a solid line stroke and several dotted-line options.

To add a stroke to a shape, follow these steps:

1. Select the shape on the slide and open the Graphic Inspector by clicking the **Inspector** button on the toolbar and then clicking the **Graphic** button at the top of the Inspector.

2. Under the **Stroke** category, choose a stroke line option from the drop-down menu.

3. Choose a color for the stroke by clicking the **color box**.

4. Use the spinner arrows or type a number to adjust the stroke size (thickness) as desired.

In Figure 5.15, I have used a solid stroke with a very thick stroke outline.

FIGURE 5.15

You can customize the stroke around a shape.

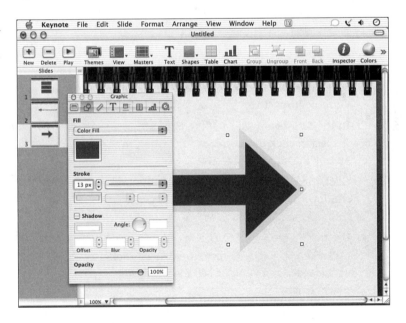

Shadow

Shadows can greatly enhance the look of a graphic. On the Graphic Inspector, you click the **Shadow** check box to enable this feature. At this point, you can change the color of the shadow and adjust the angle and the offset, the blur, and the opacity of the shadow. Simply adjust these values to make the shadow look the way you want. Figure 5.16 shows an example.

FIGURE 5.16

You can use the Graphic Inspector to add and adjust a shadow.

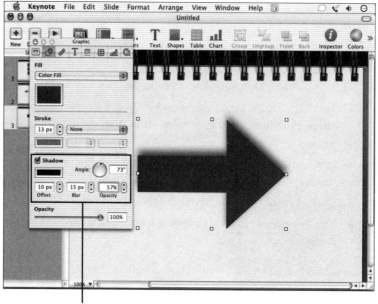

These options adjust shadow properties.

To create a shadow, follow these steps:

1. Select the object on the slide and open the Graphic Inspector.

2. In the **Shadow** section of the Graphic Inspector, click the **Shadow** check box to enable the shadow options.

3. Click the **Color** box and choose the desired shadow color from the Colors dialog box that appears.

4. Use the **Angle** wheel to change the direction of the shadow. As you move the wheel, look at the slide, and you can see the shadow's placement.

5. Adjust the **Offset**, **Blur**, and **Opacity** values as desired. You can experiment with these values and see how they affect your graphic.

note

You can adjust the opacity of a graphic by using the slider bar at the bottom of the Graphic Inspector. The opacity is the transparency of the graphic, and adjusting the opacity can be really handy when you have a number of graphics on one slide and you want a more tailored look.

Working with Images

In many cases, you might want to import photos to Keynote and use them on your slides. Photos work great for a number of presentations, especially when you are describing something physical that you can show your audience members in a photo.

Importing Photos

You can import most major digital photo file formats, including PICT, GIF, TIFF, and JPEG. You can also import photos from a PDF file. As you can imagine, this gives you a lot of flexibility without having to jump through a bunch of digital photo hoops for compatibility purposes.

You can also import photos directly from iPhoto by simply dragging them from iPhoto to your slide on Keynote. Or you can just drag a photo to Keynote, and Keynote will create a new slide within the current presentation.

If you need to import photos that do not reside in iPhoto, click **Edit**, **Place**, **Choose**. Then browse for the photo you want to include and click **Place**. The photo is imported to your slide in its full resolution, which is most likely going to be too big. So your first action is to resize the photo to an appropriate size.

caution

If you use a selection handle other than one in a corner, however, you'll distort the image. If you accidentally distort the image, just choose **Edit**, **Undo**.

Resizing Photos

You can resize a photo in a couple ways. First, you can select the photo and locate the selection handles. By using a corner selection handle, you can drag the photo to decrease or increase its size (see Figure 5.17).

FIGURE 5.17
You can drag the selection handles to resize a photo.

You can also change the size of a photo by using the Metric Inspector. Click the **Inspector** button on the toolbar and then click the **Metric** button at the top of the Inspector to open the Metric Inspector. As you can see in Figure 5.18, you can change the size of a photo by typing a size or using the spinner arrows. Checking the Constrain Proportions check box makes sure the photo adheres to a proportional size, which is a good idea unless you want it to be out of proportion to get a special effect. Also note that you can manually change the location of a photo by using the X and Y Position options (but it is easier to just drag the photo). You can also rotate the photo or flip it around by using the options at the bottom of the Metric Inspector.

FIGURE 5.18

You use the Metric Inspector to change the size of a photo.

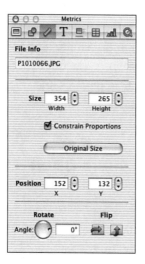

Working with Alpha Channels

Another cool photo feature in Keynote concerns masters that contain photo alpha channels. An *alpha channel* is an area on a slide that contains a transparent field so you can insert your own pictures. To use an alpha channel, click the **Masters** button on the toolbar and choose a master that contains an area for a photo. Then simply drag your photo into the photo area field and click the **Front** and **Back** buttons on the toolbar. This causes the photo to snap into the transparent field provided on the master. As you can see in the example in Figure 5.19, my photo now looks as though it appears in the photo frame, as the way you would see in a scrap book. All this with just a few clicks and a little dragging!

FIGURE 5.19

Alpha channels that are built into some slide masters give you smooth options for photo display.

Using Keynote's Image Library

You are free to import your own images, as described in the section "Using Photos in Presentations." Keynote also gives you some images that you are free to use in your presentations. Here's how you access them:

1. Select **File**, **Open Image Library**. The Image Library, as shown in Figure 5.20, contains several key files, such as Chart Colors, Flags, Objects, Pictures, and Symbols & Borders.

2. Double-click one of these files to open it. You can now see the images available within that library.

FIGURE 5.20

You can use Keynote's Image Library to access helpful images.

Another Keynote window appears, and in it you see the objects that are available in your selection. For example, in Figure 5.21, I have opened **Pictures.key** and selected a photo. I can now select **Edit**, **Copy**, go back to my presentation slide, and select **Edit**, **Paste** to put the object on my presentation. Then, all I have to do is resize the image and work with it just as I would with any other image. Make sure you peruse the files in the Image Library because Keynote provides some really nice images and graphics that you can use!

FIGURE 5.21

After you select an image and select Edit, Copy, you can paste the image into your presentation.

Using Alignment Guides to Precisely Position Text and Objects

Positioning text and objects on a slide has the potential to be a real pain. After all, without some help, it can be very difficult to get objects to line up the way you want and positioned in the right places on your slide. Don't worry, though. Keynote gives you a feature that helps you get objects placed correctly: You can use *alignment guides* to make placement work really easy.

Working with Alignment Guides

Alignment guides are a cool little feature of Keynote that can help you get an object positioned in the right place on a slide. In short, the alignment guides take the guess work out of positioning an object. For example, let's say that you want an arrow positioned exactly in the center of a slide. The alignment guides can help you do just that, and the following steps show you how:

1. Create a new slide and then choose **Masters**, **Blank**.

2. Choose **View**, **Show Rulers**. (You do not have to use the Rulers feature to use the alignment guides, but I want you to use the rulers here for illustration purposes.)

3. Click the **Shapes** drop-down menu on the toolbar and choose the arrow. You can make any size and fill adjustments you like. Your slide should now look similar to the example in Figure 5.22.

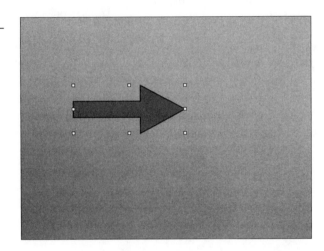

4. To put the arrow in the vertical center of the slide, drag it up or down so that it lines up with the 0 in the vertical ruler. When this is in line, a yellow alignment guide will appear, as shown in Figure 5.23. This yellow alignment guide tells you that your image is aligned in the vertical center of the slide.

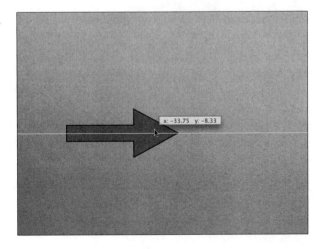

5. To put the object in exactly the center of the slide (both vertically and horizontally), simply drag the arrow until you see both vertical and horizontal alignment guides, as shown in Figure 5.24. If you use the rulers as a guide, you see that both guides fall on 0, which is the vertical and horizontal center of the slide.

What if you want to align a series of objects, such as three arrows, on a slide? The alignment guide can help you do that easily and quickly. Just create the arrows and drag them into position. When the arrows are lined up, the yellow alignment guide appears over them, as shown in Figure 5.25. It's that easy!

> **tip**
>
> There might be times when you are moving objects around and the alignment guides are distracting to you. In this case, just hold down the ⌘ key while you drag the object, and the alignment guide will not appear.

FIGURE 5.24

You drag the arrow into exactly the center position by using the alignment guides.

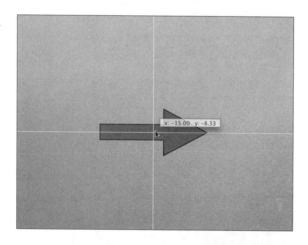

FIGURE 5.25

You can easily align objects by using the alignment guides.

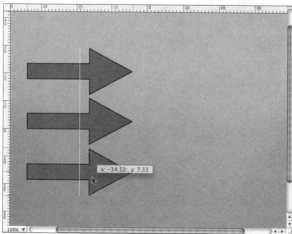

Creating New Alignment Guides

Keynote allows you to create your own alignment guides. Why would you want to do that? If you are working on a slide that has a lot of different components, or maybe several different graphics, you might want to create alignment guides to help you keep everything looking nice and even.

To create your own alignment guides on a slide, do the following:

1. Choose **View**, **Show Rulers**.

2. Position your mouse on a vertical or horizontal ruler in the desired location and then click and drag it onto the slide. A vertical or horizontal alignment guide is created.

3. Drag the alignment guide to exactly the location you need it, using the rulers as guides.

As you can see in Figure 5.26, I have made several alignment guides for this slide.

The alignment guides you create stay on the slide unless you remove them. However, the alignment guides do not actually appear in the presentation when you play it; they are provided as a help when designing the presentation only.

FIGURE 5.26

You drag from a position on a ruler to create a new alignment guide.

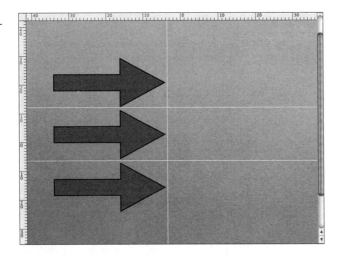

Changing the Appearance of Alignment Guides

By default, alignment guides appear in yellow, and the guides appear at the object's center. You can make a couple changes to this behavior if you like. For example, you can change the color of the alignment guides and you can also have the guides appear at the object's edges. You change these features by using Keynote Preferences. Just select **Keynote**, **Preferences**, and the Preferences dialog box appears, as shown in Figure 5.27. Click the color well to change the alignment guides color and use the "Show guides at object center" and "Show guides at object edges" check boxes as desired.

FIGURE 5.27

Make any desired changes to the Alignment Guides portion of the dialog box.

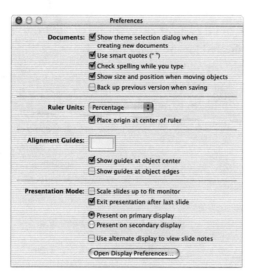

Grouping Objects

If you are using several objects on a slide and you want to work with them as one unit, you can group the objects together. This allows you to move the objects around and work with them as though they were a single image, which can be really helpful when you have several objects that are intricately placed.

Grouping and ungrouping are quite easy. To group objects, hold down the ⌘ key and select each object that you want to group. Then simply click the **Group** button on the toolbar, as shown in Figure 5.28. The objects are then grouped together. You can ungroup the objects by simply clicking the **Ungroup** button on the toolbar.

FIGURE 5.28

You can use the Group feature to work with objects as a single group.

FIGURE 5.28

You can use the Group feature to work with objects as a single group.

Working with Graphics

Now that you have some basics under your belt, you can begin creating highly effective slides using graphics and text. As the old saying goes, practice makes perfect, so don't be afraid to experiment and try new things. The following sections help you get started and show you some fun ways to use graphics.

Combining Images and Shapes

You can combine images and shapes on a slide in any way that you like. As always, you need to keep the message you are presenting at the forefront of your mind as you make decisions about how to design your slides. The good news is that you have a lot of flexibility. For example, take a look at Figure 5.29.

In this example, I have used an alpha channel on a master slide so that my photo fits inside the frame. All I did was drag the photo to the frame, resize it a bit, and then use the Front and Back buttons on the toolbar to snap the photo into the frame. Then I added an arrow object and used the Graphic Inspector to fill the object with an ocean image that matches the photo. Then I simply selected the arrow and selected Edit, Copy and then Edit, Paste to make duplicates of the arrow. I then put each arrow in the corner and held down the ⌘ key to drag them around for correct rotation. That's all there is to it!

Figure 5.30 shows another example of combining shapes and images.

FIGURE 5.29

You can combine shapes and images.

FIGURE 5.30

You can use shapes and images, shadows, and fills for a nice effect.

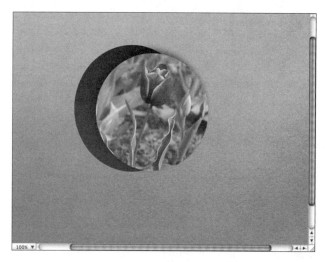

In this slide, I used two circle shapes. I filled the first with an image, used no border, and added a shadow. Then I added another circle, put it in the back of the first by using the Back button on the toolbar, and then positioned it until I was happy with the result. Then I selected the second circle and opened the Graphic Inspector so that I could use a gradient fill on it. Again, with just a few minutes of work, I came up with an interesting graphic.

Let your imagination soar! With just a few easy tools that Keynote gives you, you can create all kinds of interesting perspectives and looks for your slides.

You are free to use as many photos on a page as you like. You need to resize them and move them around to the correct positions, but you are basically free to design them in any way you like. Of course, you should always strive for graphics that are visually pleasing and easy for audience members to view.

As you work with combining images, be sure to keep in mind the opacity option, which is found on the Graphic Inspector. For example, take a look at the slide shown in Figure 5.31.

FIGURE 5.31

You can use multiple images and effects to create outstanding slides.

Pretty cool, huh? Here's how I made it. First, both of these images came from Keynote's Image Library. I simply copied the first image, the photo of the road, onto my slide. Then I copied the second, the speed limit sign onto the slide. I then selected the speed limit sign and resized and positioned it over the first image. Next, I opened the Graphic Inspector and used the Opacity slider bar to greatly decrease the opacity of the speed limit sign. Finally, I made a few more positioning tweaks, and that's it!

One last example of using shapes and images together is shown in Figure 5.32.

This slide uses the same principle as the one in Figure 5.31. I simply used two images from the Image Library, positioned the dollar sign over the other image, and adjusted the opacity.

Keep in mind that opacity can be used in a number of interesting ways. You can use opacity and other features to make some stunning visual slides for your presentations.

FIGURE 5.32
As you can see, a few editorial changes make a big difference!

Using Graphics and Text

The same basic principles apply to graphics as to text. You can add to a slide any graphic that you like and then simply create a text box for the text. Then you enter your text, adjust the size and font as desired, and position the text with the graphic. You can use opacity on either the text or the graphic, as shown in Figure 5.33.

FIGURE 5.33
Opacity settings can greatly affect graphics and text.

The Absolute Minimum

Graphics add a lot of value to presentations. As you work with graphics, keep in mind the following points:

- Make sure that graphics enhance your presentation and make your message easier to understand. Do not add graphics simply for the sake of adding graphics.

- Add shapes using the Shapes button on the toolbar, and then use the Graphic Inspector to adjust those shapes as needed.

- You can add your own digital photos or grab images from the Image Library, which is found by selecting Edit, Open Image Library.

- You can combine shapes and images, shapes and text with photos, or just about any combination you want. Remember that you can use the opacity feature in the Graphic Inspector to create stunning effects.

IN THIS CHAPTER

- Change slide backgrounds and colors
- Use the opacity setting to create exciting backgrounds
- Use alignment guides to keep things straight
- Add music to a presentation
- Add video to a presentation

6

WORKING WITH BACKGROUNDS AND MULTIMEDIA

This chapter takes a look at doing more with a presentation. Specifically, it looks at how to alter the backgrounds and colors of slides, revisits the opacity and transparency tools, and shows some ways to really put those tools to work. This chapter also takes a look at how to use audio in a presentation and also how to use video clips with Keynote.

Changing Slide Backgrounds and Colors

Keynote gives you plenty of slide templates to choose from. You can get even more templates from a number of Internet sites as well (see Appendix C, "Helpful Keynote Web Sites"). However, what if you want to change the slide background and color? You can! In fact, you can actually create your own template from scratch so that your entire presentation uses your custom background and colors. You'll find out how to do that in Chapter 10, "Extending Keynote."

But what if you only want to change a few slides within an existing presentation? For example, let's say you are giving a presentation about your company to new employees. However, your company recently purchased another company across town. You want to devote a few of your slides to the new company, but you want to make sure you keep the two companies separate in the audience's mind. One way you can do this is to alter the theme background for the slides that are about the other company. You don't have to do anything radical, but the different background can help the audience transition from the main focus of your conversation. You'll give the audience a verbal transition, of course, but the slide background can help give your audience a visual transition as well.

So, when should you change the background on a set of slides within a presentation? You should use this technique only if you are talking about a subset of something within a presentation. You should not randomly change the background on the slides for visual interest because that tends to make your presentation look choppy. Always think in terms of using a subset of slides for content that really needs to be set off from the other content.

You can change the slide background in two easy ways. First, you can simply edit the particular slide and change the background as you wish. In other words, you can change the slides you want without having to create new master slides or integrating two different presentations together. Second, you can use two different themes within the same presentation. The following sections show you how to change slide backgrounds in these two ways.

Using the Slide Inspector to Change a Background

The Slide Inspector gives you options for changing the type of layout for the text on a slide, changing a slide's background color or type of background, and deciding whether a transition is used between one slide and the next.

The Slide Inspector has a drop-down menu that lets you choose the type of background you want. You can choose from Color Fill, Gradient Fill, Image Fill, and None. Depending on what option you choose, the Slide Inspector changes so that you can configure the option. For example, if you pick Gradient Fill, the Slide Inspector gives you color boxes so that you can choose the colors for the gradient, and then you have the option to choose the angles and positioning of the gradient.

The final part of the Slide Inspector is the Transition section, which is covered in Chapter 8, "Exploring Transitions and Builds." We won't get into those options here.

To change the background of a slide, just follow these steps:

1. Select the slide that you want to change in the **Slides pane**.

2. Click **Inspector** on the toolbar.

3. On the Inspector, click the **Slide** button. As you can see in Figure 6.1, the Slide Inspector gives you an easy way to quickly make changes to the slide background and colors.

FIGURE 6.1

You can easily change the slide background by using the Slide Inspector.

4. Click the **Master & Layout** drop-down menu to select a different slide configuration, as shown in Figure 6.2. This gives you an easy way to change the title and bullet options for the particular slide without any affecting the whole presentation.

5. If you want to show the title on the slide and show the body text formatting (for example, bullets), check the **Show Title** and **Show Body** check boxes. If you do not want to show this information, clear the check boxes. These options can be helpful because you can choose a Title & Bullets layout and still have the ability to customize it by using the Show Title and Show Body check boxes.

FIGURE 6.2

You use the
Master &
Layout drop-
down menu to
choose other
slide
configurations.

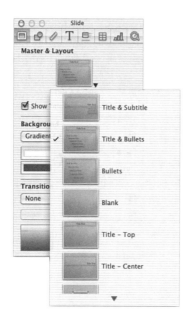

6. Choose a background type from the Background drop-down menu.

   ■ If you choose **Gradient Fill**, select a color and an angle for the gradient.

   ■ If you choose **Image Fill**, you'll see a preview box for the background and buttons so that you can choose the image you want to use.

   ■ If you want to use a color fill, choose the appropriate option from the **Background** drop-down menu (see Figure 6.3). Click the color selection box and then choose a color from the background from the Colors dialog box that appears.

7. When you're done making selections in the Slide Inspector, click the red **Close** button in the Slide Inspector.

Changing the Background by Combining Themes

The second way to change the background of a slide is to actually use two different themes in one presentation. There's a really easy way to do that. For example, let's say that you want to create a subset of slides that use a different theme—perhaps something similar to your main presentation theme but different enough for contrast purposes. Because you want to work with two different themes, the easiest way to create the presentation is to create your main presentation and then do the following:

1. Click the **New** button and choose a new theme. Another presentation is created.

2. In the new presentation, create the desired slides (which will be the subset within the main presentation), using this new theme.

3. When you are done, simply drag the new slides to the original presentation, as shown in Figure 6.4. The imported slides retain their theme formatting without affecting any of the original theme slides.

FIGURE 6.3

You can click the color selection box below the Background drop-down menu to choose a color for the background.

FIGURE 6.4

You can drag slides that have different themes applied to them from one presentation to another.

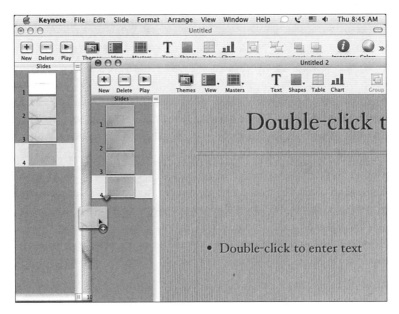

As you can see, you now have the original presentation with a subset of slides that use a different theme. It's that easy!

Adding Visual Interest to Objects by Using the Opacity Setting

I've made mention in the past couple chapters about opacity. *Opacity* is an image term that simply refers to the transparency, or "see-through-ness," of an object. The more opacity an object has, the less see-through it is, and the less opacity an image has, the more transparent it is. For example, in Figure 6.5, the object on the left has 100% opacity, and the object on the right has 22% opacity. As you can see, the object on the right is rather transparent.

FIGURE 6.5

Opacity determines how transparent an object looks.

Opacity is a very helpful feature of Keynote because it allows you to customize the way images look on a Keynote slide, and it gives you a way to introduce interesting textures. For example, take a look at the slides in Figure 6.6. All the effects you see were created simply by placing objects on a slide and adjusting the opacity of those objects as desired.

The example shown in Figure 6.6 contains basic text, using the default theme's font and style. I've simply added the arrows, which diminish—that is, become less and less opaque—down the page. Diminishing objects can really help draw attention to certain items on a slide and give your slide a graphics boost for additional visual interest.

FIGURE 6.6

The opacity set-
tings create a
diminishing
effect on this
slide.

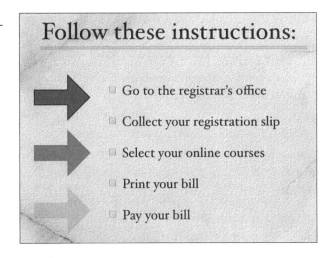

To create a slide with diminishing arrows, follow these steps:

1. With your desired slide open, click the **Shapes** drop-down menu and choose the arrow option (see Figure 6.7). An arrow appears on the slide.

FIGURE 6.7

You can click
the Shapes
menu and
choose the
arrow shape.

2. Move the arrow to the desired position and resize it as necessary (see Chapter 5, "Working with Graphics," for details).

3. Make sure the arrow is selected and then click the **Inspector** button on the toolbar and choose the **Graphic** button on the Inspector.

4. Change the color fill, stroke, and shadow as desired (see Chapter 5 for details).

5. Keep the opacity set to 100%.

6. Choose **Edit**, **Copy** and then choose **Edit**, **Paste**. A copy of your arrow appears on the slide.

7. Position the second arrow as desired and then go back to the Graphic Inspector and set the opacity for this arrow to around 58%.

8. Repeat steps 6 and 7, but set the opacity of the third arrow to 15%. This isn't an exact science, so feel free to adjust the opacity values in the previous steps to suit your needs.

That was fun and easy! You can use this process on any type of object or picture to give your slide some additional visual interest.

Another example of using opacity to add visual interest is shown in Figure 6.8. This example uses a background picture from the Image Library. I simply put the image on the slide and then adjusted the opacity to a very low percentage. The image is still visible, but it doesn't dominate the slide, leaving me room to do work with text. Many times, your images may work great as a background, but they tend to overwhelm the slide if you don't tone them down with the opacity feature.

FIGURE 6.8

Use the Opacity setting to add visual interest to the elements in your presentation.

The following steps outline the basic process you follow to create a slide like the one shown in Figure 6.6:

1. On the desired slide, click the **Masters** drop-down menu on the toolbar and choose the **Blank** option.

2. Choose **File**, **Open Image Library** (see Figure 6.9).

FIGURE 6.9

The Image Library gives you a wealth of images and objects you can use in presentations.

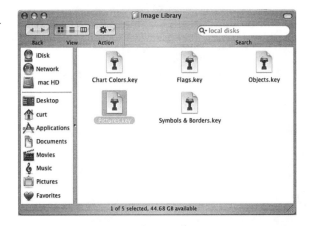

3. In the Image Library window, double-click **Pictures.key**. The Image Library opens.

4. Locate the desired picture in the Slide Organizer and select it. The image appears on the Slide Canvas.

5. Click the picture to select it and then choose **Edit**, **Copy**.

6. Close the Image Library.

7. Back in your presentation, choose **Edit**, **Paste**. The picture now appears on your slide. Resize the picture as necessary so that it covers the slide (see Chapter 5 for more details).

8. Make sure the picture is selected and then click the **Inspector** button on the toolbar and choose **Graphic** button on the Inspector.

9. Change the opacity to a low percentage, such as 20%. Close the Graphic Inspector.

10. Click the **Text** button on the toolbar to insert a text box. Type the wording you want to appear in the slide and then select **Format**, **Font** to change the size and style of the wording as desired. See Chapter 2, "Working with Text," for more information about working with text.

As you can see, opacity gives you a quick and easy way to make an image work for a slide background. But that's just the beginning! There is still more you can do with opacity settings.

The slide shown in Figure 6.10 uses the same image twice to create another type of effect. I got the stopwatch from the Keynote Image Library, simply enlarged it on the background and rotated it to the left, and then adjusted its opacity so that it is barely visible. Next, I pasted the image to the slide again, adjusted the positioning, and rotated the second image to the right by using the Metrics Inspector. This approach creates a slide that is interesting and professional looking.

The example shown in Figure 6.11 uses a process that is somewhat similar to the earlier example of the diminishing arrows. This time, however, you stack the images one on top of the other, with the highest-opacity image on top and the lowest-opacity image on the bottom. This gives the illusion of movement.

As you can see, there are many different things you can do with opacity. All the examples you just looked at were made by simply positioning objects and using the Opacity slider bar on the Graphics Inspector. No other tricks were used at all!

Using Audio in a Presentation

Working with audio naturally leads to the issue of usage. How should you use audio in a presentation, or should you use it at all? That is an important point to consider, and just because you *can* use audio in a Keynote presentation doesn't necessarily mean that you *should*.

As with all other things in a presentation, you should think carefully before you use audio—for two major reasons. First, if you are using the Keynote presentation in a live presentation, the audio portion may have to be miked so that all the audience members can hear it, depending on the size of the room in which you are speaking. This issue can be a problem in some locations.

Second, and more importantly, does the audio help your message? You might need to play an audio file to support your slide or show an example, but superfluous audio files do not work well. For example, have you ever watched a Keynote or PowerPoint presentation where the speaker put little sound effects throughout the slides (hands clapping, bells ringing, and so on)? What did you think? All too often, these tactics seem more like a gimmick than anything else. My advice is to be very cautious when you use audio. Make sure the audio really has a purpose and always ask yourself, "Is the audio helping or distracting from my message?"

note

If you have problems stacking images and getting them in the right order, use the **Front** and **Back** buttons on the toolbar to get the correct stacking effect.

tip

Opacity can really give your slides a smooth look, and it can help you control the overall appearance of slides. Don't let this helpful tool slip into the background of your mind as you are working with Keynote!

Importing Audio Files

Just as you can import different kinds of photos and image files into Keynote, you can also import sound files. Specifically, Keynote supports AIFF and MP3 sound files. If this is a bunch of gibberish to you, don't worry.

AIFF files are uncompressed, digital audio files. They are very close to the files that are on any music CD you purchase. *MP3* files, on the other hand, are compressed music files that are specifically designed for computers because they take up less storage space on a hard disk. Here's the skinny: AIFF files sound great, but they eat up a lot of disk space. MP3 files sound almost as great, but they use only a fraction of the disk space that an AIFF file uses.

So how can you get these files and how can use them in Keynote? It's easier than you might think:

■ You can drag any song from your iTunes library to a slide in Keynote. iTunes stores your songs as either AAC or MP3, so there are no compatibility issues. Your iTunes library is usually found in [Home]/Music/iTunes/iTunes Music. If it makes your life easier, just open iTunes and directly drag a song from iTunes to your desktop and then drag the song to the Slide Canvas.

■ You can download MP3 files from the Internet and drag them to your slide. As long as the file is an MP3 file (and almost all sound files from the Internet are), everything will work just fine. The cool thing about this option is that you can find all kinds of sound effects, or "sound bites," as they are often called. Check out www.sound-effects-library.com or www.thefreesite.com to find a bunch of sound effects. Also, you can just search for *MP3 files* at any search engine, such as www.google.com, to find many additional sites.

■ You can put a music CD into your Mac's CD-ROM drive, open the CD, and simply drag the file from the CD to your Keynote slide. Note, however, that the AIFF format is used with this method. That's fine, but just be aware that the AIFF file will greatly add to the overall file size of your presentation.

> **note**
>
> You can use downloaded songs and sounds in live presentations without worrying about copyright. This is considered "fair use." However, if you create a slideshow that will be used for marketing purposes, put on a CD, or sold to people in any way, you need to have permission to use the sound files. Check out the Web site where you downloaded the songs or sounds to find out more about specific copyright issues.

Adding an Audio File to a Slide

Now that you know how you can find audio files to add to a presentation, let's walk through putting the link to the song into a slide.

To add audio from iTunes to a slide, follow these steps:

1. Select the desired slide in your Keynote presentation so that it appears on the Slide Canvas.

2. Open iTunes. It is probably an icon on the Dock, but if it is not there, select **Macintosh HD**, **Applications**, **iTunes**.

3. Find the song in the iTunes library and then drag it to your desktop. Or you can just directly drag it to the Slide Canvas, as shown in Figure 6.12.

The song appears on the slide as an audio icon, which you can see in Figure 6.13. When you play the slide, the music will automatically play.

tip

When you drag a song from iTunes, the song is copied to the desktop or the Slide Canvas. Your original song stays safe and sound in your iTunes library, so don't worry.

Now, if the audio icon perplexes you a bit, don't worry. The audio icon simply tells you that a music file is attached to the slide. The icon does not appear when you actually play the slide. You can drag the audio icon around if you like and place it anywhere on the slide (so that it is out of your way), but keep in mind that the audio icon doesn't actually do anything except tell you that there is an audio file attached to the slide.

You can double-click the audio icon to hear the music play, and if you later decide that you do not want to use the audio on the slide, you just select it and select **Edit**, **Delete**. This does not delete the song from iTunes or wherever you originally imported it from; it just removes it from the slide.

FIGURE 6.12
You drag a song from the desktop to the Slide Canvas.

Using the Media Inspector to Adjust Audio Options

One issue to keep in mind as you use audio in presentations is simply how the audio feature works. When you advance to a slide that has an audio file, the audio file begins playing. In the case of a song, the file stops playing at the end of the song or when you advance to the next slide. You can't place a single audio file across a whole presentation (for example, to have music playing in the background while you talk); the audio is limited to a slide-by-slide basis.

FIGURE 6.13
The audio now appears as an icon on the slide.

However, you can adjust the audio volume and repeat option (which can cause the audio file to play over and over as long you linger on the slide). To set these options, click the **Inspector** button on the toolbar and then click **Media** button on the Inspector. The Media Inspector appears, as shown in Figure 6.14.

FIGURE 6.14
You can use the Media Inspector to adjust slide media.

By default, the audio file does not repeat, but you can cause it to by clicking the **Repeat** drop-down menu and choosing **Loop** or **Loop Back and Forth** (which plays the audio forward and then plays it in reverse).

You can adjust the overall volume of the audio playback by simply moving the **Volume** slider bar.

Finally, notice the controls at the bottom of the Media Inspector. These controls allow you to play the audio file while you are working on it.

Using Video in a Presentation

Keynote supports both the QuickTime movie format and Flash for video, and to use video in a presentation, all you have to do is drag a movie to your slide. Of course, it is beyond the scope of this book to explore the process of making movies, but your Mac provides a really cool program called iMovie that you can use to make movies and even photo slideshows. Then you can export the movies to the QuickTime format and then simply drag them to the Slide Canvas.

After you drag a movie to the Slide Canvas, you see the first frame of the movie. As with any object, you can use the selection handles to resize the movie window and to drag the movie window around to position it on the screen in a desirable place. You can use text or anything else on a slide with the movie, as shown in Figure 6.15.

caution

When you place a sound file on a slide, the sound file still resides on your computer, not within Keynote itself. So, if you copy a Keynote presentation to a CD or to another computer, you must copy the audio file as well.

tip

To get some detailed help with using iMovie, see Chapter 17, "Making Digital Movie Magic with iMovie," in *Special Edition Using Mac OS X, v10.3 Panther.*

FIGURE 6.15
You can position a movie as needed.

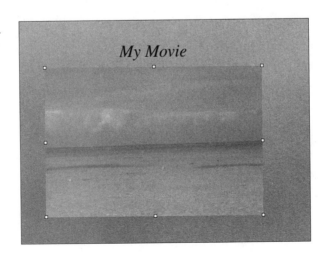

My Movie

I don't mind telling you that Keynote doesn't do a great job with large movie windows. When you play such a movie, it will look rather grainy, so smaller movie windows work best.

As with audio, you can use the Media Inspector to adjust the repeat behavior and sound of a movie. You can also use the Poster Frame slider bar, shown in Figure 6.16, to choose a frame of the movie that is visible in the movie window on the slide until you start playing the movie. By default, the first frame is shown, but you can simply adjust the Poster Frame slider value to choose the frame you want to show.

tip

Remember to use the alignment guides to line everything up, if necessary.

FIGURE 6.16

You can move the Poster Frame slider bar to choose the frame you want displayed until the movie begins.

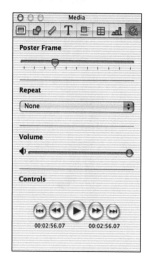

note

Although you can't control movie playback, you can use a Keynote feature called a build to determine when the movie appears on the slide during the slideshow. If that sounds both interesting and confusing, don't worry; we'll talk about builds in Chapter 8.

As with audio files, a movie begins playing as soon as you advance to a slide that contains a movie. The movie stops playing when the movie ends or when you advance to the next slide. Unfortunately, there are no controls for the movie during playback. In other words, during the presentation, you cannot pause or stop the movie so that you can make comments.

note

As with an audio file, a movie file is external to a presentation. So, if you copy the Keynote presentation to a CD or move it to another computer, you must also copy the movie file as well, or the movie will not play during your presentation.

The Absolute Minimum

With just a few tricks, you can make Keynote presentations look really great. Keep these points in mind:

- You can change slide backgrounds by using the Slide Inspector. You can also mix and match themes by simply dragging slides from other presentations to the Slides pane.

- You can set the opacity on the Graphic Inspector to manage the transparency of images. This simple tool gives you many creative options.

- You can use the alignment guides to help align images and objects. Don't forget that you can also create your own!

- Audio and movie files can really add some cool features to a presentation. You can use them as needed by simply dragging them to the Slide Canvas.

IN THIS CHAPTER

- Use Keynote views to make your work easier
- Manage the slide order in a presentation
- Keep things organized with slide groups
- Keep things a secret with skipped slides
- Make speaker notes to help remember the details
- Spell check a presentation and more

7

MANAGING PRESENTATIONS

Your slides can be a great help, but they can also throw a presentation off track if you are not careful. Why, you might ask? The answer is simple. As you work with Keynote, it is easy to get so interested in the details of each slide that you do not stop to consider the entire presentation. It is not unusual for people to circumvent this part of the planning process, but the overall order, look, and feel of a Keynote presentation is of utmost importance to a presentation's success. This chapter examines some important issues related to the management of a presentation.

Working with Keynote Views

Keynote provides three different views that can make your work easier as you put together presentations. The views are Navigator, Outline, and Slide Only, and as you'll quickly see, these views are designed to help you work with Keynote more effectively. It is important to realize that the different views don't actually *do* anything. They simply organize information in a way that is best for you to work with. Also, you can switch between views as you like without affecting anything that you have done in the presentation. The main idea to keep in mind here is simply that views are designed to help you view a presentation in a way that is useful as you are creating it.

Navigator View

Navigator view is the default view Keynote uses. In Navigator view, you see a graphical representation of each slide in the Slide Organizer. When you click a slide in the Slide Organizer, the slide contents appear on the Slide Canvas, where you can then work with the slide in any way that you like (see Figure 7.1).

FIGURE 7.1

Navigator view gives you an icon of each slide in the Slide Organizer.

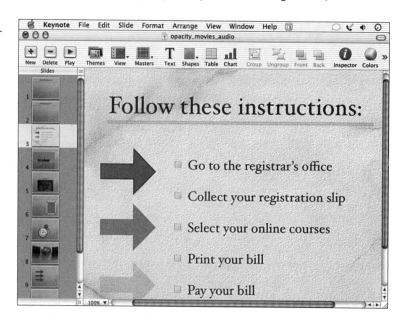

Navigator view works great for slides that primarily have a lot of graphics. However, what if a presentation presents a lot of data, which you have displayed in a simple bullet text format? Navigator view isn't very helpful because it is basically impossible to read the content on the different slides in the Slide Organizer. In Navigator view, you have to guess which slide is which and click around through them to see what appears on the Slide Canvas.

Outline View

Rather than play the guessing game, you can switch to Outline view to view data-heavy slides. Select **View**, **Outline**, and the Slide Organizer changes to an outline view, as shown in Figure 7.2. In Outline view, you see a small slide icon for each slide, but you see all the text that is written on the slide, including any bullet points or other text on the slide. Outline view is, well, an outline of the presentation, right before your eyes! As you are looking through the presentation, this view can really help you get a solid feel for the content and the way it is ordered in the presentation.

FIGURE 7.2

Outline view helps you see the text content of each slide.

Slide Only View

You can access Keynote's Slide Only view by selecting **View**, **Slide Only**. This option simply removes the Slide Organizer so that you see only the currently selected slide, as shown in Figure 7.3. This is a quick way to view slides without the distraction of the Slide Organizer. The cool thing is that you can quickly move from Navigator view or Organizer view to Slide Only view and back again by using the View menu.

FIGURE 7.3

Slide Only view can give you a quick and unencumbered look at one slide at a time.

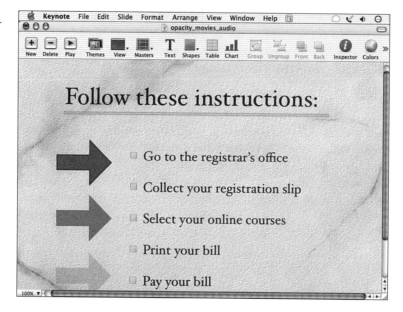

Rearranging Slide Order

Let's face it; no one is perfect. No matter how hard you might try, things can get out of order. You might be on Slide 10 of a presentation and discover that you need to add a new slide between Slides 2 and 3. Or perhaps you have already created a Keynote presentation and you later find that you want to reorganize the whole thing. You can relax. Keynote makes it very easy to rearrange your slides.

The Slide Organizer is your best friend in these circumstances, and all you have to do is simply drag slides to move them around. You can also insert slides at any point in the presentation.

First of all, let's say you want to move a slide around to a different location in your presentation. Simply click the slide in the Slide Organizer and drag it to the desired location, as shown in Figure 7.4. You can drag slides in either Navigator view or Outline view.

You can also drag multiple slides at the same time. For example, let's say you create three slides but later decide that those slides need to be moved, as a group, to a different location in the presentation. No problem. Just hold down the ⌘ key and click each slide to select it. Then drag the slides to the new location, as shown in Figure 7.5.

FIGURE 7.4
You can simply drag a slide to a new location in the Slide Organizer as needed.

FIGURE 7.5
You can drag a group of slides in the Slide Organizer to change the order of a presentation.

Aside from dragging slides around in the Slide Organizer, you can also insert or delete slides at any time. To insert a new slide, in the Slide Organizer simply select the slide that you want the new slide to follow and then click the **New** button on the toolbar. The new slide appears. Similarly, you can select a slide and click the **Delete** button on the toolbar to remove it from the presentation.

tip

Oops! Did you delete a slide by mistake? No problem. Just select **Edit, Undo Delete**.

Grouping Slides

As discussed in Chapter 1, "Beginning Skills: Getting to Know Keynote," you can group slides together in the Slide Organizer. If that idea intrigues (or perplexes) you, you've come to the right place.

First of all, let me say that grouping slides doesn't do anything to a presentation. The slides still play in the same order and in the same manner, and as far as the audience is concerned, grouping doesn't mean anything at all. So if grouping doesn't affect a presentation, what's the point? The point is simply to help you. Think of slide grouping as a tool that can help keep you organized as you work with slides in the Slide Organizer.

Let's say you are giving a presentation at your company about three different products. For each product, you have an introductory slide and about five slides concerning the product. To help you keep the slides straight, you can group the five or so slides under the introductory slide so that you can easily locate the appropriate set of slides for each product in the Slide Organizer. Once again, this doesn't do anything to your presentation when it comes to viewing the slideshow, but grouping can help you stay more organized and keep things straight as you work on the slides.

tip

Rather than use the **Tab** key, you can drag a slide to the right in the Slide Organizer to group it.

How do you group slides? The process is quick and easy. Just follow these steps:

1. In the Slide Organizer, select the first slide in the group.
2. Press the **Tab** key. Note that the slide indents below the previous slide, as shown in Figure 7.6.

FIGURE 7.6

You select a slide and press the Tab key.

3. Repeat this process for the additional slides in the group. Note that slides you want to group must be in consecutive order before you can group them.

4. A disclosure triangle now appears beside the slide under which the new grouped slides reside. You can click the triangle to hide the slides in the grouping and click it again to disclose them, as shown in Figure 7.7.

After you group slides together, you are not stuck with the grouping. You can easily remove a slide from a grouping by simply dragging it back to the lineup of slides so that it is not indented. At this point, the slide is no longer grouped. If you need to ungroup a collection of slides, just select them by holding down the ⌘ key and dragging to the left. You can also hold down the **Shift** key and press the **Tab** key to ungroup the slides.

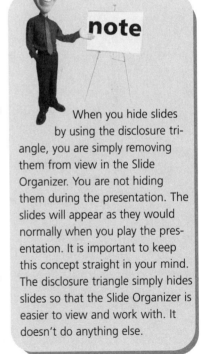

note

When you hide slides by using the disclosure triangle, you are simply removing them from view in the Slide Organizer. You are not hiding them during the presentation. The slides will appear as they would normally when you play the presentation. It is important to keep this concept straight in your mind. The disclosure triangle simply hides slides so that the Slide Organizer is easier to view and work with. It doesn't do anything else.

FIGURE 7.7
You can use the
disclosure trian-
gle to view or
hide a group of
slides.

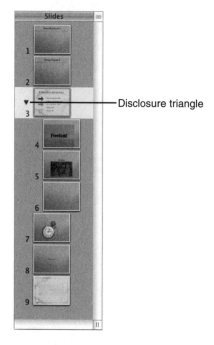

Disclosure triangle

One other grouping trick you can use is to group
within a group. Let's say you have a group of
three slides. However, you want to have another
group of two slides under the last slide in the
first group. What can you do? Just drag the
slides to the right to create a secondary group,
as shown in Figure 7.8. You can group as many
levels as you like. Just make sure you keep
things organized in a way that is useful to you.

tip

Don't confuse the Group
and Ungroup buttons on the
toolbar with grouping slides.
The Group and Ungroup
buttons are used to group
objects on a slide (such as
shapes). They are not used
to group and ungroup slides in
the Slide Organizer.

FIGURE 7.8

FIGURE 7.8

You can create groups to as many levels as you need.

Skipping Slides While Viewing a Slideshow

Let's say you have created a 30-minute sales presentation with Keynote. The sales presentation presents all aspects of a product, and you travel around to different customer sites, making this presentation. However, some customers allow you only 15 minutes for the presentation. Of course, you could speed things up and work through the Keynote presentation more quickly than usual, or you could simply create a new, scaled-down presentation, or…

As you might guess, there is a better way. Keynote gives you the option to skip slides during a presentation. You use the Slide Organizer to determine what slides you want to skip, and when you play the Keynote presentation, those slides are simply skipped over and do not appear. This is a great way to reduce the length of a presentation without having to create an entirely new one.

For example, let's say that you have several primary slides about a sales product. You also have several grouped slides under those that go into more detail. To shorten the presentation, you can skip the extra slides that contain the additional information. As you can imagine, this trick is a great way to tailor an existing presentation to your time needs, or even the needs of the audience, without any additional labor on your part. All it takes is a few mouse clicks.

To skip a slide when viewing the slideshow, follow these steps:

1. In the Slide Organizer, select the slide you want to skip.

2. Select **Slide**, **Skip Slide**. The slide now appears as a collapsed slide in the Slide Organizer, as shown in Figure 7.9.

Notice that the slide numbering adjusts to reflect the skipped slide. The little bar you see between Slides 3 and 4 simply notes a skipped slide, but the skipped slide is not numbered.

FIGURE 7.9

The skipped slide now appears collapsed in the Slide Organizer.

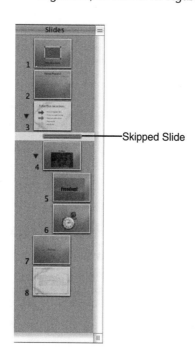

Skipped Slide

3. To stop the slide from being skipped, select it again and select **Slide**, **Don't Skip Slide**.

Working with Master Slides and Layouts

As you have been working with Keynote, you have probably accessed master slides and layouts on those slides from time to time. Master slides may seem a bit daunting and confusing at first, but in reality, master slides exist to make Keynote much easier to use. In a nutshell, master slides give you a slide layout so that all you have to do is type the information or insert the content you want. This keeps you from having to stare at a blank slide and create your own slide content from scratch.

Master slides exist to make Keynote easier to use, give you a smooth slide look and layout, and make your work with Keynote faster and more productive.

As you know, you can access master slides by clicking the **Masters** button on the toolbar. As shown in Figure 7.10, you see an icon view of each master slide that is available, and all you have to do is click the desired master slide to see a new slide appear on the Slide Canvas.

FIGURE 7.10

You can click the Masters button to choose a master slide.

What master slides should you use and when? That depends on your needs. If you are not sure what the master slides give you, click the **Masters** drop-down menu and take a look at the names of the master slides. This will give you a good clue as to what you are getting. Also, keep in mind that new master slides adhere to your current theme when you select them.

Master Slide Options

The master slide icons are a bit difficult to see, so this section provides a quick explanation of how and when you might use each one. Use the following as a quick guide to the master slides so you can see exactly what you'll get when you choose that master:

■ **Title & Subtitle**—This master slide, as shown in Figure 7.11, provides you with a title and subtitle area where you double-click to enter text.

FIGURE 7.11

You click to enter a title and subtitle.

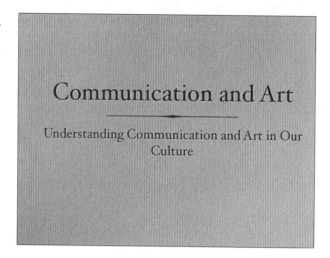

■ **Title & Bullets**—This is a standard master slide that you use to enter a title and bullet points (see Figure 7.12). You'll use this one a lot. Keynote automatically adjusts to the number of bullet points you want to type.

■ **Bullets**—This master option gives you a place to create bullet points only; there is no title. This master works well if you need to extend a bulleted list from a previous slide or if you simply do not want a title getting in the way.

■ **Blank**—As you can guess, this master doesn't have anything on the slide. All you see is the theme design, but no text boxes or other items. Use the blank master if you need to create a custom slide.

■ **Title—Top**—This option gives you a title box at the top of the slide but nothing else. This master works well if you want to use a title but create the rest of the slide content from scratch.

tip

What if you do not want a subtitle? No problem, just click to select the subtitle box (the selection handles appear) and press the Delete key. You are left with the main title only.

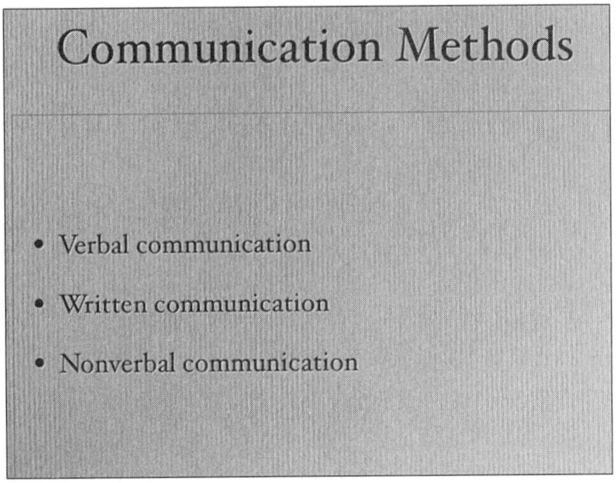

FIGURE 7.12

You click to enter a title and bullets.

Communication Methods

- Verbal communication

- Written communication

- Nonverbal communication

FIGURE 7.12
You click to enter a title and bullets.

- ■ **Title—Center**—This master is virtually the same as the Title—Top master, except that the title appears in the center of the slide. There is no subtitle.

- ■ **Photo—Horizontal**—This master, as shown in Figure 7.13, allows you to place a horizontal photo in the center of the slide and create a title beneath the photo. See Chapter 5, "Working with Graphics," to learn more about working with graphics.

FIGURE 7.13

This master gives you a photo holder and title text.

Early Tulip

- ■ **Photo—Vertical**—This master option, as shown in Figure 7.14, gives you places for a vertical photo, a title, and standard paragraph text. This is a great master to use when you need to title a vertical photo and provide a short blurb of information about it.

FIGURE 7.14

You can use this master to place a vertical photo and add a title and explanatory text.

- **Title, Bullets & Photo**—This master option is similar to Photo—Vertical, but it provides a larger title area and text box for bullet points. Use this master when you need to display a photo but provide more text on the slide.

- **Title and Bullets Left**—This option places the title at the top of the page and bullets to the left, leaving you an open area to place any other slide item you might want to include.

- **Title and Bullets Right**—This is the same as Title and Bullets Left except that the bullets are to the right of the slide instead of to the left.

Quick Access to Master Slides

There is a quick trick you might want to keep in mind as you work with master slides. You can use the **Masters** button on the toolbar to select the master slide you want to use and also have the master slides hiding directly behind the Slide Organizer. To access them, click the double-line area in the upper-right corner of the Slide Organizer and drag down (see Figure 7.15).

This moves the Slide Navigator down the screen and reveals the master slides, as shown in Figure 7.16.

note

If you want to further manipulate master slides and even create your own, check out Chapter 10, "Extending Keynote."

FIGURE 7.15
You click and drag the double line with your mouse.

FIGURE 7.16
Master slides can be accessed onscreen.

You can now easily use the Slide Organizer as well as the master slide list in a split-pane view.

Creating Speaker Notes

As a professional speaker, you should never need speaker notes, right? Ha! Even the most professional speaker or presenter has an affinity for notes. After all, the pressure and stress of any speaking or presentation event is enough to make you forget your name, much less the finer points of your presentation.

It is perfectly fine to use speaker notes when you give a presentation. In most cases, they really are a must-have. Keynote gives you a basic outline of your presentation by its nature, but what do you do with all the extra information you want to say? For example, let's say you have a slide with three bullet points. Under each bullet point are several pieces of information you want to point out but not include on the slide. This is the place for speaker notes, which are notes to you to help you remember what to say; the audience does not see them.

Speaker notes do not appear in the presentation, but you can add them to any slide and print them later for your own use. In this manner, Keynote can really be the tool you use to help prepare for an entire presentation, not just the slides for the presentation.

To create speaker notes, just select the desired slide in the Slide Organizer so that it appears on the Slide Canvas. Then select **View**, **Show Notes**. A text box appears at the bottom of the Slide Canvas, and in it you can type any note or information you want, as shown in Figure 7.17.

FIGURE 7.17

You type speaker notes in the box provided at the bottom of the screen.

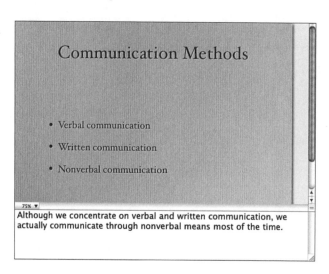

Spell Checking and Find and Replace

Misspelled words are a nightmare item for presentations. You are plugging along, really doing a great job with your presentation, and there it is: a glaring misspelled word on the screen. Unfortunately, despite all your hard word on the presentation, the spelling error makes you look unprofessional. It looks as though you didn't proof your slides and you are unprepared.

Sound drastic? I'm afraid spelling errors on slides are just that, but the good news is that they are easy to avoid, thanks to Keynote's spell checker. You can spell check a presentation and lose most of those spelling problems immediately. In fact, Keynote can even check your spelling as you type.

Before you breathe a sigh of relief, I do have word of warning. Spell checker only checks for misspelled words—not poor usage. For example, "Two bee or knot too bee" is spelled correctly, but the usage is wrong. Also, watch out for *you*, *you're*, and *your* and *there*, *their*, and *they're*. Spell checker will not find usage errors, so unless you have a degree in English, it is always a good idea to have someone else proofread your presentation. (I always do anyway, even though I have a degree in English!)

The point is that spelling errors are common, and they can creep into a presentation, but you can fix and avoid them with just a little proofing work on your part and some good help from Keynote.

Using Spell Check

When you select **Edit**, **Spelling**, you can choose from these three options:

- **Spelling**—This option checks the presentation and opens the Spelling dialog box so you can fix the errors.
- **Check Spelling**—This option scans the presentation and highlights any words that are potentially misspelled.
- **Check Spelling as You Type**—When you select this option, the spell checker checks the presentation as you type, underlining any potentially misspelled words in red. It's a good idea to turn on this feature because it can point out problems as you work.

When you select **Edit**, **Spelling**, **Spelling**, the Spelling dialog box, which points out misspelled words, appears. As you can see in Figure 7.18, Keynote tries to guess which word you are really after. If it finds the right word, you can just select it in the **Guess** box and click **Correct**, or you can simply retype it in the provided text box and then click **Correct**. What if the spell checker keeps flagging a word that is correct, such as a technical or medical term? In that case, you just click the **Forget** button so that Keynote will stop flagging it, or better yet, click the **Learn** button so Keynote can add it to the dictionary.

FIGURE 7.18

The Spelling feature suggests alternative spellings for misspelled words.

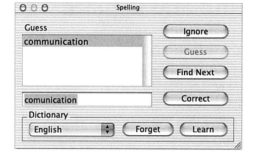

Using Find and Replace

Along with spell checking, Keynote also gives you a find and replace option. Let's say that you have created an entire presentation, which is about using a computer. Throughout the presentation, you have used the term *cat* where you should have used the computer term *mouse* (hey, it's my example). Instead of having to wade all the way through the presentation and make the corrections manually, you can have Keynote simply find all instances of *cat* and replace each one with *mouse*. Here's how you do it:

1. Choose **Edit**, **Find**, **Find Panel**. The Find dialog box appears (see Figure 7.19).

FIGURE 7.19

You can use find and replace to quickly change words or phrases throughout a presentation.

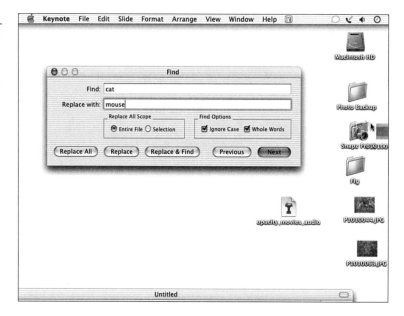

2. In the Find dialog box, type the word to find in the **Find** text box and type the word you want to replace it with in the **Replace with** text box. Note that you can check the entire file or the current selection and you can choose to ignore case and work only with whole words. In this example, selecting **Whole Words** would confine the find and replace function to only finding *cat*, rather than words that contain cat, such as *caterpillar*.

3. Click **Replace & Find** to start the replacement process. Keynote finds and replaces your entries.

The Absolute Minimum

Keynote makes the tedious work of presentations simple with a number of tools and features:

- Keynote views let you easily toggle between different view options within a presentation.
- You can use the Slide Organizer to quickly rearrange slides, work with slide masters, group slides, and create new slides.
- You can use the Slide menu to skip slides you don't want to show in the presentation.
- You can create speaker notes with the View menu.
- Keynote gives you a spell checker to check your presentation's spelling and the find and replace function to quickly and easily find and replace words or phrases in the presentation.

IN THIS CHAPTER

- Create transitions between slides
- Modify transitions in a presentation for a cleaner look
- Create effective slide content showing with builds
- Customize builds to meet your needs
- Manage builds and delivery

8

EXPLORING TRANSITIONS AND BUILDS

You know as well as I do that computer graphics are really cool. We love to watch animated things, and the Mac's graphics are so smooth and nice that working with a Mac can be more fun than watching TV.

The same concept holds true for a presentation. No matter if that presentation is in front of a live audience or if you are building an automated presentation for the Web, some animation in a Keynote presentation can really make things look sharp. In fact, it can make a presentation look really professional, like something a graphics expert put together. The good news is that you don't have to be a graphics expert to use Keynote's awesome animation features. Keynote does most of the work, and in this chapter, you'll see just how to use these features.

Using Transitions Between Slides

A *transition* between two slides is simply a graphical effect that moves the audience from one slide to the next. Sounds good, but there are a few things you need to know about using transitions before you put them to work.

First, transitions are designed to make the movement from slide to slide smoother. In the end, that's really all they do. A transition simply gives the audience something to look at as the change from one slide to the next is made. Transitions are very cool looking, and as you work with them, you'll have a tendency to get mesmerized by them. But don't! Transitions are designed to be graphical effects. But the effect of a transition shouldn't become the focus of the presentation. Therefore, you should choose a transition style that works well with your presentation, and as a general rule, you should use that same transition style throughout the entire presentation. Although it's tempting, from a public speaker's point of view, the use of different transitions throughout a presentation can be hokey and rather distracting to the audience.

The moral of the story is to find a transition you like—one that seems to work well with the mood and theme of your presentation—and then use that same transition throughout the entire presentation. This will make your presentation look more professional and polished.

On to the fun stuff! The great thing about transitions, like most everything else in Keynote, is that you need only a few mouse clicks to set one up. The following steps show you how:

1. Open a presentation. In the **Slide Organizer**, select the desired slide so that it appears on the Slide Canvas.

2. Click the **Inspector** button on the toolbar. On the Inspector, click the **Slide** button. The Slide Inspector appears. As you can see in Figure 8.1, the Slide Inspector contains an area for setting transition options.

3. Click the first drop-down menu in the **Transition** section and select a transition type. An example of the transition animation appears in the preview box in the lower-left corner of the Slide Inspector.

4. Repeat steps 1–3 on the rest of the slides in the presentation. You cannot globally apply a transition to your entire presentation, but you must set up the transition on a slide-by-slide basis.

tip

You can try several different transitions and watch the animation in the preview box on the Slide Inspector. When you close the Slide Inspector, the transition is applied to your slide.

Slide Inspector button

FIGURE 8.1

You can access
transitions on
the Slide
Inspector.

The slide will not look any different after you have closed the Slide Inspector, but
you'll see the transition in effect when you play the slideshow. Take a close look in
the Slide Organizer, and you'll see that each slide that has a transition has a little
fill mark in the lower-right corner of the slide. In Figure 8.2, the first slide has a transition applied and the second slide does not.

Transition applied

FIGURE 8.2

A slide that has
a transition has
a little mark in
the lower-right
corner.

Choosing a Keynote Transition

If you look at the various transitions available on the Slide Inspector, you see that you have several to pick from. Keynote provides modern-looking 3D transitions as well as some 2D transition effects. Table 8.1 lists the transitions that are available and gives you a quick explanation of what they do.

TABLE 8.1   Transitions in Keynote

Transition	Description
None	This is the default setting. No transition is applied to the slide. In this case, the new slide suddenly appears, replacing the old one, without any kind of graphical transition effect.
Cube	This 3D transition makes the slides look they are placed on a cube that rotates.
Flip	This 3D transition flips the old slide to reveal the new, as one would turn a poster or piece of paper.
Mosaic	With this 3D transition (which has Large and Small options), new slides build on top of the previous slides, using a mosaic pattern.
Dissolve	With this 2D transition, one slide dissolves into a new slide.
Drop	With this 2D transition, the new slide drops over the old slide.
Fade Through Black	This 2D option moves to a black screen, and then the new slide fades in.
Motion Dissolve	With this 2D transition, one slide dissolves to the next one with a bit of motion.
Move In	This 2D transition causes the new slide to slide in over the previous one.
Pivot	This 2D transition causes the new slide to pivot over the previous one.
Push	With this 2D transition, the new slide pushes the previous one away.
Reveal	With this 2D transition, the new slide is revealed as the previous one moves away.
Scale	This 2D transition races the new slide in from the middle of the previous one.
Twirl	This 2D transition causes the previous slide to twirl off the screen and the new slide to twirl onto the screen.
Wipe	This 2D transition looks as though the previous slide is being wiped off the screen while the new slide slides onto the screen.

With all these transition options, which one should you choose? That all depends on your sense of style and the style of your presentation. You should spend some time experimenting with different transitions so you can get a feel for how they work and how they will look in a presentation. Also, avoid using the most graphic of the bunch just for the sake of "coolness." For example, the Twirl transition is a cool graphic effect, but it tends to get old quickly. In most cases, it is best to stick with a transition that looks good but one that is not overly graphic. As you work with transitions, keep the term *enhance* in your mind. Transitions should always enhance a presentation, not dominate it.

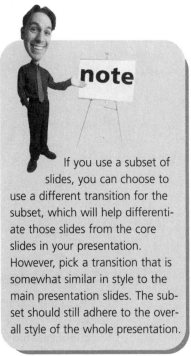

If you use a subset of slides, you can choose to use a different transition for the subset, which will help differentiate those slides from the core slides in your presentation. However, pick a transition that is somewhat similar in style to the main presentation slides. The subset should still adhere to the overall style of the whole presentation.

Changing Transition Effects and Speed

You can make changes to the settings of some transitions. For example, if you use the Cube transition, you can determine the cube speed, which is how fast the cube rotates from one slide to the next, and you can also change the orientation of the movement, such as from top to bottom, bottom to top, left to right, and right to left. Some transitions, depending on their nature, do not allow you to change the orientation, some do not allow you to change the speed, and some do not allow you to change anything at all. The settings are available in the Slide Inspector only if they can be changed.

To change a transition's effect or its speed, just follow these steps:

1. Open the desired presentation and select a slide that has a transition.

2. Click the **Inspector** button on the toolbar and then click the **Slide** button. The Slide Inspector appears.

3. In the **Transition** area of the Slide Inspector, click the second drop-down menu to change the behavior of the animation and use the **Speed** slider bar to change the speed, as shown in Figure 8.3. The box in the lower-left corner of the Slide Inspector displays each change you make.

4. Repeat steps 1–3 for the other slides that have transitions applied.

FIGURE 8.3

You can change the orientation and speed of the transition.

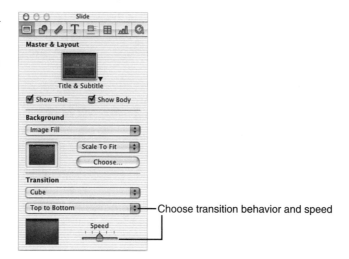

Choose transition behavior and speed

What Are Builds?

Builds are probably one of the most important features of Keynote. A build has the power to control information that you present to the audience and provide very nice graphical features.

What is a build? A *build* is a graphical effect in which different elements can appear on the slide when you want them to. In other words, a build graphically builds the slide in front of the audience's eyes. Builds work on objects, such as text, charts, tables, and images. You can totally manage the way the builds work and even apply builds to groups of images. For example, let's say that you want to show the audience a pie chart. Instead of just having the pie chart appear as one item, you can have each wedge of the pie fly in and build the pie chart as you talk about each piece. As you can imagine, builds give you a very clever and cool way to graphically dress up your slides.

However, builds also have a greater purpose. As you are talking about a particular slide, audience members have a tendency to read ahead of you. Let's go back to the pie chart example. Let's say you are using a pie chart such as the one shown in Figure 8.4.

As you can see, this pie chart has six pieces. If you simply display the pie chart on the screen, audience members will start examining all of the chart, even though you might be talking about only the first piece of the pie. In this situation your audience members' minds might wander away from what you are saying and focus on the whole picture, rather than the piece you want to them to focus on.

One of the cool things about builds is that they can help you control the audience's focus. Rather than show them the whole pie chart, you can bring in one piece at a time. This "hiding" of information helps keep the audience focused on you, the subject at hand, and your message. You can also use this approach with images, tables, and text.

FIGURE 8.4

Pie charts make effective build elements.

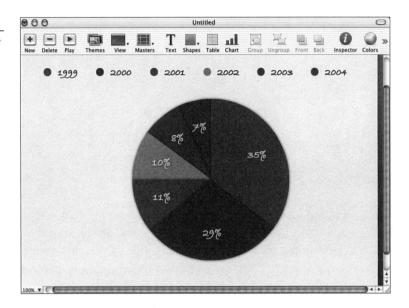

So, builds provide a cool graphical feature, but they can also help you give a stronger presentation, which is the whole reason you are using Keynote in the first place.

At first glance, builds might seem intimidating. After all, they require a lot of work, right? Like all things with Keynote, builds are not complicated to make, once you get a few basic skills down.

Getting Familiar with the Build Inspector

As you might guess, you create builds by using the Build Inspector. Before we start actually creating some different builds, let's take a moment to get familiar with the Build Inspector and how it works.

First, select any slide and then click the **Inspector** icon on the toolbar. Then click the **Build** button. The Build Inspector appears. As you can see in Figure 8.5, the Build Inspector gives you a look at the slide and a Build In and Build Out tab.

Parts of builds appear as you click the mouse. When you show a slide, you can choose for it to at first show nothing at all; then as you click the mouse on your presentation, each piece appears on the screen, thus creating the build. In the middle of the Build Inspector is the "First build requires click" check box, which you should keep checked so that you have control over the first build.

FIGURE 8.5

You use the
Build Inspector
to create slide
builds.

On the Build In tab, you can determine how the build is going to work. The options include Build Style, Order, Direction, Delivery, and Speed. When you use the Build In tab, the items in the build are added to the slide as you click your mouse.

If you use the Build Out tab, shown in Figure 8.6, you have the same options, but the build occurs in reverse. You start with a complete slide, and as you click your mouse, the items in the build are removed from the slide. This feature works well if you want to show your audience the big picture of something and then break the concept down into pieces.

FIGURE 8.6

The Build Out
tab allows you
to create reverse
builds.

As you can see, the Build Inspector is easy to use, just like the rest of Keynote. By using this simple tool, you can create effective builds no matter what slide content you want to work with. The following sections show how to create builds for a variety of slide content.

Text Builds

Let's say you have a slide that has five bullet points. Sure, you can simply show your audience members the slide without any intervention, but as human nature would dictate, the audience members are going to read ahead of you as you talk. Because you may not want audience members to read the fifth bullet while you are talking about the first, you can create a text build for the bullets. This way, each bullet point appears only when you click your mouse and are ready to talk about it.

To create a text build, follow these steps:

1. Select the desired slide in the Slides Organizer so that it appears on the Slide Canvas.

2. Click the **Inspector** button on the toolbar. Click the **Build** button. The Build Inspector opens.

3. On your slide, click the bullet points so that the text box around them becomes visible.

4. On the **Build In** tab on the Build Inspector, choose a build style. The build style determines how the bullet points will appear. You can simply choose to have them appear, or you can use some graphical effects to have them appear, such as drop, flip, pivot, and twirl.

5. In the **Delivery** drop-down menu choose **By Bullet**, as shown in Figure 8.7.

FIGURE 8.7

You can choose the By Bullet option in the Delivery drop-down menu.

Choose a delivery option

6. View the effect you want on the slide preview window at the top of the Build Inspector. Use the Speed slider to adjust the speed of the build as desired (see Figure 8.8).

FIGURE 8.8
You can use the Speed slider to adjust the speed of the bullet points' entry on the slide.

Because you are only creating a text build, which is a single build item, you don't have to worry about the Order drop-down menu. Finally, don't worry that all the bullets come in one after the other on the sample slide. Keynote is just giving you a preview. When you play the presentation, you'll have to click your mouse for each bullet to appear onscreen.

Finally, what do you do if you want the bullet points to leave the screen as you talk about them instead of build them to the screen? In this case, you use the Build Out tab instead of the Build In tab. This causes your bullets to appear all at once, and as you talk about them, you can click your mouse to have them exit the screen. The Build Out tab gives you the same options as the Build In tab, so just select the Build Out tab and follow the previous steps.

Table Builds

You can easily create table builds. This is a great way to keep your audience members organized and stop them from reading ahead.

You can build a table in two ways. First, you can build the entire table at one time. This is helpful with a slide that has several items, including a table. You can talk about the other items and then have the table build at one time with a nice build style. Or you can have the table build one piece at a time, or even one row or column at a time. The choice is completely up to you, and you can do it all with the Build Inspector. The table build delivery options are listed in Table 8.2.

TABLE 8.2   Table Build Delivery Options

Delivery Option	Description
All at Once	Moves the entire table onto the screen at one time.
By Row	Moves the table onto the screen one row at a time.
By Column	Moves the table onto the screen one column at a time.
By Cell	Moves the table onto the screen one cell at a time.
By Row Content	Moves the empty table onto the screen and then fills in each row.
By Column Content	Moves the empty table onto the screen and then fills in each column.
By Cell Content	Moves the empty table onto the screen and then fills each cell, one at a time.

Follow these steps to create a table build:

1. From the Slide Organizer select the slide that contains the table for which you want to create a build.

2. Select the table on the slide.

3. Click the **Inspector** button on the toolbar and then click the **Build** button. The Build Inspector appears.

4. On the Build Inspector, choose an option from the **Build Style** drop-down menu. Depending on your selection, you might also be able to choose a direction from the **Direction** drop-down menu.

5. Use the **Delivery** drop-down menu to choose the kind of delivery you want, such as all at once, by row, by column, or by cell (see Figure 8.9). This determines the way your slide builds. Be sure to watch the sample window so you can see a preview of how the slide will be built. Remember that when you play the presentation, you'll build each portion of the slide by clicking your mouse.

caution

Be wary of using the By Cell options with a big table. Because you have to click to get each individual cell onto the screen, the process can get tedious. For large tables with a lot of content, the By Column or By Row options work best.

Chart Builds

You can build a chart just as easily as you can build a table, and charts are particularly effective with build patterns. Because charts are graphical anyway, chart builds can really give a presentation the edge you are looking for, and they can help control the information in the chart so that it is presented at the time that you want your audience to see it.

FIGURE 8.9

You choose the manner in which a table will be built.

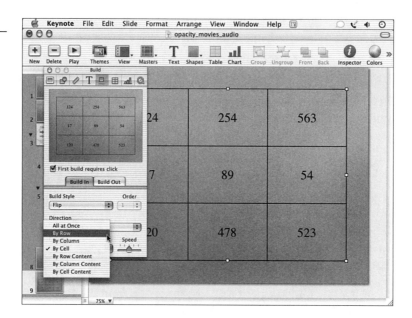

When you create a chart build, you can choose from several options for the actual delivery of the chart build (see Table 8.3).

TABLE 8.3   Chart Build Delivery Options

Delivery Option	Description
All at Once	Moves the entire chart onto the screen at one time.
Background First	Moves the chart axes onto the screen, followed by the data elements (such as bars, lines, and area shapes) at once.
By Series	Moves the chart axes onto the screen and then the data elements, one full set at a time.
By Set	Moves the chart axes onto the screen and then each separate data element, one series at a time.
By Element in a Series	Moves the chart axes onto the screen and then each separate data element, one at a time.
By Element in a Set	Moves the chart axes onto the screen and then each separate data element, one set at a time.

To create a chart build, follow these steps:

1. From the Slide Organizer select the slide that contains the chart for which you want to create a build.

2. Click the chart that you want the build applied to.

3. Click the **Inspector** button on the toolbar and then click the **Build** button. The Build Inspector appears.

4. Choose a build style for the chart from the **Build Style** drop-down menu. Depending on your selection, you might also be able to choose a direction from the **Direction** drop-down menu.

5. Using the **Delivery** drop-down menu, choose the kind of delivery you want (see

Figure 8.10). (Refer to Table 8.3 for an explanation of the options.) Your selection here determines the build of your slide. Be sure to watch the preview window so you can see a preview of how the slide will be built. Remember that when you play the presentation, you'll build each portion of the slide by clicking your mouse.

> **tip**
>
> Again, think carefully and experiment with the build options. The By Series and By Set options work great. Also, keep in mind that you can play your presentation and see exactly how it will look, and you can then return to the Build Inspector at any time to make any changes you want. Make sure you resave your presentation after you make changes.

FIGURE 8.10

You choose the delivery option you want to use on a chart.

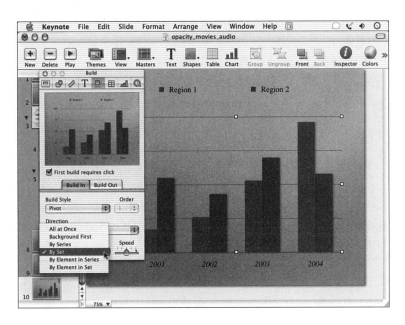

Image Builds

There isn't anything special about image builds. In fact, to create one, all you have to do is select the desired image and access the Build Inspector. You can then choose the build style, direction (if applicable), and speed to determine how and how quickly the image builds. As you can see in Figure 8.11, the clock twirls into place. Good enough, you might think, but what do you do when you have several different items on a slide that need to build? How do you control the build order, or what if you want them to build as a group? The next section shows you how.

FIGURE 8.11
You can build images to a slide just as you can any other object.

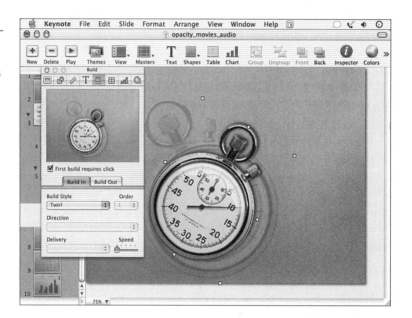

Creating Multiple-Build Slides

Creating builds is easy when you're working with one build item on a slide, but what if you have more than one? Also, what if you need some items to build at the same time? This seemingly complicated task really isn't difficult.

For example, take a look at the sample slide in Figure 8.12.

Let's say that you want to build each item on the slide, including the slide title, and you want to control the order of those builds. Once again, you use the Build Inspector. Just follow these steps:

1. Select the desired slide.

2. Click the **Inspector** button on the toolbar and then click the **Build** button. The Build Inspector appears.

FIGURE 8.12
A slide can con-
tain several ele-
ments.

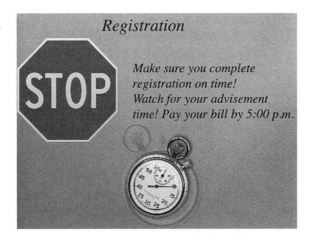

3. Select the first element on the slide that you want to build.

4. Choose the build style for the first element by using the **Build Style** drop-down menu (see Figure 8.13). Adjust the **Speed** slider as desired. Don't worry about the Order option at the moment.

FIGURE 8.13
You choose build
options for one
element at a
time.

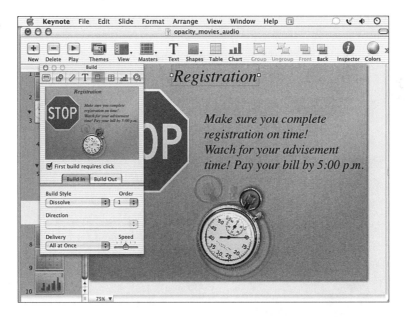

5. Continue this process for each additional build element on the slide.

6. When you have applied the builds, you can determine the order. (The build order refers to the order in which the elements appear on the slide.) On your

slide, select the first item you want to build, and then on the **Build Inspector**, click the **Order** drop-down menu and choose **1**. Then select the next item on the slide that you want to build. Click the **Order** drop-down menu on the Build Inspector and click **2**. Repeat this process for each build item until you have them all ordered in the way you want the slide to build.

7. When you are done choosing a build and making adjustments to the settings, play the slide and click through the order of the build to make sure everything works as it should.

As you can see, building multiple items on the same slide is easy because Keynote gives you the power to control the build order. However, what if you need two different items to build at the same time? Let's say that you want the Stop sign and the text to build at the same time. In this case, you must group the items first and then apply the build. Here's how you do it:

1. On the desired slide, hold down the ⌘ key and click the items you want to group. In Figure 8.14, the Stop sign and the text are selected.

Multiple items are selected

FIGURE 8.14
You select the elements you want to group.

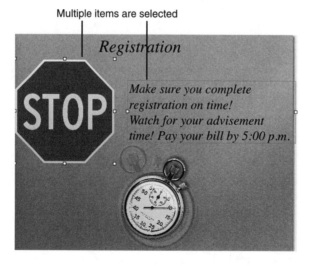

2. Click the **Group** button on the toolbar. The selected items become one group.

3. Open the Build Inspector and choose the desired options from the **Build Style** and **Direction** drop-down menus, and adjust the **Speed** slider as needed. As you can see from the preview window, the items build at the same time because they are a group.

tip

Keep in mind that if you later ungroup the items, the build will not work correctly. Also, if you group certain items together, some build styles may not be available to you. For example, if you have a pie chart with a legend grouped, you can no longer have the individual pieces of the pie delivered one at a time.

THE ABSOLUTE MINIMUM

Transitions and builds can really add a lot of polish and control to presentations. Keep these points in mind:

- You can quickly apply transitions to slides by using the Slide Inspector. Just use the drop-down menu and choose the transition you want.

- For some transitions, you can adjust the behavior of the transition and the speed. You can make these changes on the Slide Inspector.

- You use the Build Inspector to create builds on slides, using all kinds of objects, including text, images, charts, and graphs.

- You use the Order option on the Build Inspector to manage slides with multiple build items. You can also build several items at the same time by grouping them.

- Create a slideshow with Keynote slides

- Create QuickTime and PDF presentations easily with Keynote slides

- Print presentations for a variety of purposes

- Use presentation hardware and projectors with a Mac

9

VIEWING AND PRINTING A PRESENTATION

All the hard work has finally paid off. You are now ready to show your stuff and make a presentation! But wait, what do you want to do, exactly? Do you need a live presentation, a QuickTime movie, a PDF printout? Do you need to create speaker notes and even print copies of your presentation for audience members?

No problem! You can do all these things with a Keynote presentation. In this chapter, you'll see how to actually use the Keynote presentation you have spent so much time preparing.

Viewing a Slideshow

Of course, the reason you create a Keynote presentation is so that someone else can view it, whether that viewing is in a live presentation manner where you talk about the slides or in some automated format. The odds are quite good that you are preparing a Keynote presentation for onscreen viewing, which simply means that you are going to show your presentation to a live audience.

When you play a presentation, you control the advancement of the slides with your mouse or with a few keys on the keyboard.

To play a slideshow, just do this:

1. Make sure no slide is selected in the Slide Organizer and then click the **Play** button on the toolbar.

2. When you play the show, use your mouse, press the **spacebar**, or use the **right arrow** and **down arrow** keys to advance the slideshow.

3. Use the **up arrow** or **left arrow** keys to go back to the previous slide.

4. Press **Esc** or **Q** to quit the slideshow.

You might also be able to use a wireless remote with a Mac so that you can advance to the next slide without staying glued to the computer. Most of the remotes available use USB ports, and overall, they work great. You can find out more about wireless remotes for a Mac at any computer store that sells Apple products, or you can check out the Keyspan presentation remote at

www.keyspan.com/products/usb/presentationremote.

If a slide is selected in the Slide Organizer when you click the Play button, the slideshow will start with the selected slide.

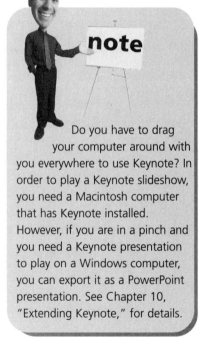

Do you have to drag your computer around with you everywhere to use Keynote? In order to play a Keynote slideshow, you need a Macintosh computer that has Keynote installed. However, if you are in a pinch and you need a Keynote presentation to play on a Windows computer, you can export it as a PowerPoint presentation. See Chapter 10, "Extending Keynote," for details.

Slideshow Viewing Preferences

Aside from simply playing a slideshow on a Mac, there are a few other viewing options that you should note. In Keynote, select **Keynote**, **Preferences**. The **Presentation Mode** section of the Preferences dialog box, shown in Figure 9.1, has the following options:

FIGURE 9.1

You can use the Preferences dialog box to control slideshow playback.

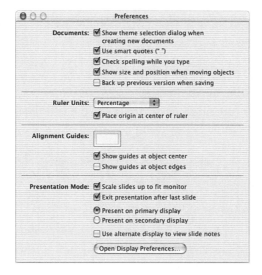

- **Scale slides up to fit monitor**—When you check this check box, the slides scale up to fill the entire monitor screen. This can be helpful, but you might want to experiment with it a bit. If you have used low-resolution photos or movies in the slideshow, they become grainy or distorted looking when you scale them up. Make sure you experiment with this option to see if everything looks okay before you use this option to show the presentation to a live audience.

- **Exit presentation after last slide**—When this check box is selected, the presentation closes when you click your mouse or press the spacebar after the last slide. It returns you to the Keynote application. This option is selected by default, but if you don't want Keynote to exit the show (even if you click), simply uncheck this check box. From a speaker's point of view, it is a good idea to uncheck this option and not return to the application at the end of the presentation because that simply looks a bit unprofessional. Your best bet is to stay on the final slide or, better yet, go to a black screen.

- **Present on primary display** and **Present on secondary display**—
  These two radio buttons allow you to control where the presentation is
  played. You can play it directly on your Mac's display, or if you are connecting
  another screen or projection device, you can set the show to play on the
  secondary display. (You'll see how to set up a secondary display later in this
  section.)

- **Use alternate display to view slide notes**—This is a cool option that
  allows you to see your slide notes on an alternate display. For example, let's
  say that you have your Mac set up by a podium. You configure Keynote to
  show the slideshow on a secondary display, such as a projection screen. If you
  use this option, your slide notes appear on your Mac screen rather than on
  the presentation. This can be a handy way to use your notes, but use caution!
  Often, printed notes are much easier to use, so make sure you practice with
  the onscreen notes option before using it in front of a live audience.

So, what if you want to show a slideshow on a secondary display? In many cases,
this is exactly what you'll need to do. You might connect your Mac to a projector
that displays your slideshow on a large screen or possibly even another kind of
large-format screen that connects to your Mac.

You can connect a secondary display and quickly set it up by using the Displays
preference in the System Preferences dialog box. Then you simply tell Keynote what
to do with the display by following these steps:

1. Choose **Apple**, **System Preferences**.

2. Click **Displays** (see Figure 9.2).

FIGURE 9.2

You use the
System
Preferences dia-
log box to access
displays.

3. Click the **Arrangement** tab and follow the onscreen instructions to select the display. If you do not see an Arrangement tab, your system does not support a dual-monitor configuration.

4. In Keynote, choose **Keynote**, **Preferences**. The Preferences dialog box appears.

5. Select the **Present on secondary display** button. Close the Preferences dialog box.

You can now play your slideshow and see it on the secondary display.

tip

Your Mac might support video mirroring, which displays the same video signal to both your Mac's display and the secondary display. This allows you to see your slides at the same time as they are displayed to the audience. See your Mac documentation for details.

Creating a QuickTime Presentation

QuickTime is the movie format standard for the Mac, and indeed, it has become increasingly popular for most other computer platforms. QuickTime movies are commonly used on the Internet, and there are QuickTime versions for Windows computers so that anyone can watch a QuickTime movie.

Keynote gives you the ability to easily export a presentation to the QuickTime format. You then end up with a QuickTime movie of the slideshow that can be used in a number of ways:

■ You can create an interactive slideshow that people can watch from a kiosk or a computer that does not have the Keynote software installed. The viewer watches the slideshow and clicks a mouse or presses the spacebar to advance the movie. You can also create the movie so that it is automated and simply plays over and over, without any human intervention.

■ Using the QuickTime format, you can choose a file size for a movie. This allows you to export the slideshow in full quality or reduce its size so that you can burn it to a CD or use it on the Web.

■ Because the slideshow is exported in the QuickTime format, you can even import the QuickTime slideshow into iMovie and further edit it by adding other video clips, sound, effects, and so on. You can even use iDVD to burn the slideshow to a DVD so that it can be watched on any standard DVD player.

Before you export a slideshow to QuickTime, think about how you'll want to use it, such as onscreen, on the Web, burned to a CD, and so on, because Keynote will give you those options during the export process. When you are ready to export a movie, just follow these steps:

caution

Make sure you edit and review a presentation carefully before you export it. After you export a presentation to QuickTime, you cannot edit the QuickTime movie. In order to fix a mistake, you have to return to Keynote, fix the problem, and then export the slideshow again.

1. In Keynote, open the presentation you want to export and then select **File**, **Export**.

2. In the drop-down window that appears, choose the **QuickTime** radio button, as shown in Figure 9.3, and click **Next**.

FIGURE 9.3

You can export a slideshow to QuickTime.

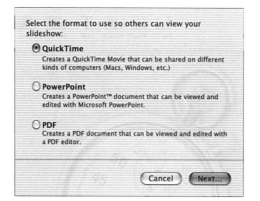

3. In the next drop-down window that appears, you can choose the playback control and the format, as shown in Figure 9.4. Click the **Playback Control** drop-down menu to choose either **Interactive Slideshow** or **Self-Playing Movie**. If you choose Interactive Slideshow, the viewer must click his or her mouse or spacebar in order to advance the movie. Also if you choose Interactive Slideshow, you can choose to change the **Slide Duration**, **Build Duration**, and **Repeat** options. Under the **Repeat** drop-down menu, you can choose from **None**, **Loop**, and **Back and Forth**.

note

By default, slides are configured to show for 10 seconds, and each build duration takes 3 seconds. You can change these defaults if you like in the Playback Control options of the export process, but the defaults work well for most purposes.

FIGURE 9.4

You can choose a playback control and format.

4. Under **Formats**, you can choose the following:

   ■ Full Quality, Large

   ■ CD-ROM Movie, Medium

   ■ Web Movie, Small

   ■ Custom

   If you choose **Custom**, a Custom QuickTime Settings dialog box appears, as shown in Figure 9.5, where you can determine the video size and whether you want to copy audio. Choose the video size and audio feature you want. You can also click **Settings** in either the Video section or the Audio section to open a settings window, as shown in Figure 9.6. In this settings window, you can select the overall features and quality. As a general rule, the default options are fine, but you should experiment with them a bit in order to tweak the quality and movie-watching experience. When you are done, click **OK** to continue.

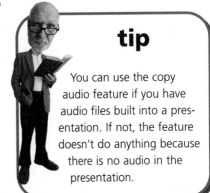

tip

You can use the copy audio feature if you have audio files built into a presentation. If not, the feature doesn't do anything because there is no audio in the presentation.

5. In the next window that appears, shown in Figure 9.7, give the movie a name and choose where you want to save it by using the drop-down menu. When you are done, click the **Export** button.

FIGURE 9.5

You can choose custom settings.

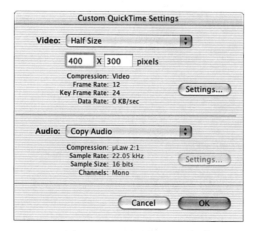

FIGURE 9.6

You can choose quality and motion settings.

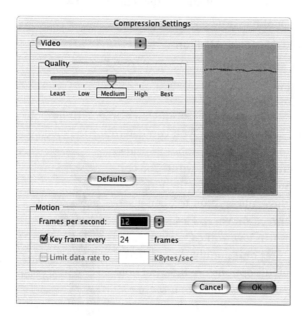

FIGURE 9.7

You enter a name for the movie, choose a location, and click Export.

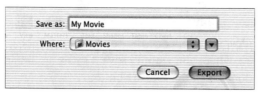

Keynote exports all the slides in the movie, and you end up with a QuickTime presentation. Just double-click the QuickTime file to watch it.

Exporting to PowerPoint is covered in Chapter 10.

Creating a PDF File of a Presentation

PDF, or Portable Document Format, is a standard file format made popular by Adobe and viewable using the free Adobe Reader, which is installed on your Mac by default and is also available at www.adobe.com. PDF has become the standard document format because it does such a great job of displaying text and graphics. With the proliferation of the Internet and downloadable files, PDF has become the document format of choice. It is universally readable on different platforms and operating systems and generally works great.

Keynote gives you the ability to easily export a Keynote presentation as a PDF document. Using Adobe Reader, anyone on any kind of computer and using any operating system can then read the presentation. If you are using the full version of Adobe Reader, you can even edit the PDF of the presentation.

Why would you want to export to PDF anyway? Here are some common scenarios:

- You can use a PDF file to share a presentation with others across different operating systems and platforms. Although when it is a PDF file, the presentation is not a slideshow, it still contains all your information and slide content. Furthermore, it can be easily printed.

- By making a presentation into a PDF file, you can post the presentation on the Web or email it to others. Because the PDF format is a standard, anyone using the free Adobe Reader can open it.

- You can collaborate with others. Those who use the full version of Adobe Reader can edit and work with the presentation in any way they like.

note

Keep in mind that Keynote has to export everything to QuickTime, which includes all the slide objects, transitions, builds, and so on. For this reason, the amount of time that it takes to export the presentation will vary from presentation to presentation, depending on the features used.

note

Any changes made to the PDF are simply made to the PDF file. You have to manually make those changes again to the Keynote presentation itself if you want to update the actual presentation. In other words, you can't automatically transfer the PDF edits back into the actual Keynote presentation.

As you can see, there are several reasons you might want to export a presentation to a PDF file, and the good news is that the export process requires only three steps:

1. Select **File**, **Export**.

2. In the drop-down window that appears, choose the **PDF** radio button and click **Next**.

3. In the next drop-down box that appears, enter a name for the file and choose a place to save it. Click **Export**.

Your Keynote presentation is converted to a PDF file.

Printing a Presentation

When you think of Keynote, you most likely think of an onscreen presentation, and after all, that's a great reason to use Keynote. However, you might not realize up front that Keynote also gives you some very nice printing capabilities. What if you are giving a presentation to a group of people, and you want to send them home with your presentation? What if you need to create speaker notes? What if you want the audience to have your slides and your speaker notes? No problem! You can use Keynote to print all these items with just a few mouse clicks.

Keynote allows you to print slides, using several different printing options, or you can simply print an outline of the presentation. Either way, the printing process is quick and easy, and you end up with good-looking printouts.

First, if you simply want to print the outline, select **File**, **Print Outline**. The standard print dialog box appears, and in it you can choose the number of copies you want. Keynote then prints the outline view of the slides, just as you would see if you chose to view the Slide Organizer in Outline view.

To print the slides themselves, you select **File**, **Print Slides**. Once again, this opens the standard print dialog box, shown in Figure 9.8. If you are using more than one printer, make sure you click the Printer drop-down menu and choose the printer you want to print to.

FIGURE 9.8

You use the Print dialog box to decide what you want to print.

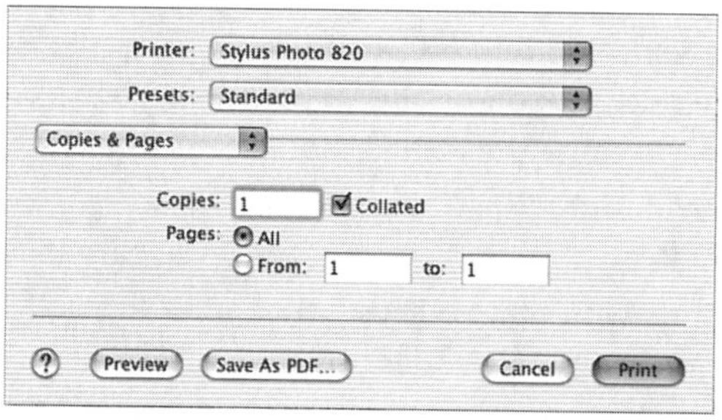

However, before you click the **Print** button, you have some options you need to check out. You can click the **Copies & Pages** drop-down menu and select **Keynote**, as shown in Figure 9.9.

FIGURE 9.9

You can choose Keynote from the Copies & Pages drop-down menu.

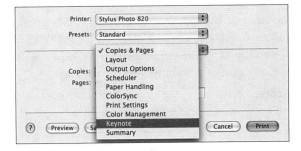

This changes the print dialog box to include some Keynote-specific options, as you can see in Figure 9.10.

FIGURE 9.10

You can choose from the available Keynote print options.

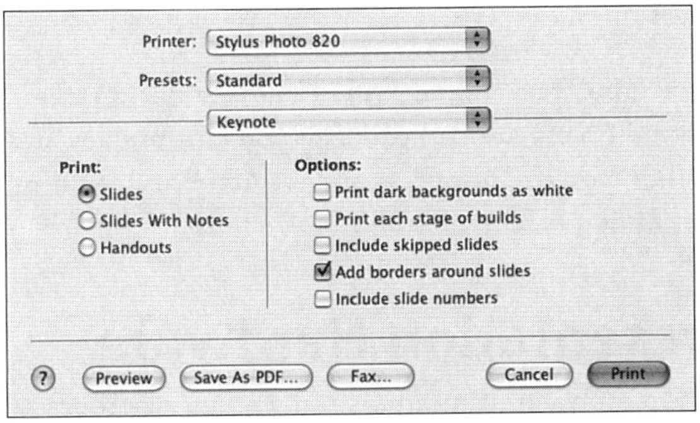

Under **Print** you can select from the following:

- **Slides**—This option prints all the slides, one per page. You can configure Keynote to use a number of print options, which are described in the following bulleted list.

- **Slides With Notes**—This option prints each slide on a sheet of paper but includes any slide notes you have created under the slides. You have the same additional printing options that you have when you choose the Slides option.

- **Handouts**—This option creates audience handouts by printing four slides to a page. Speaker notes are not printed when you print handouts, but you have the same additional printing options that you have when you select the Slides option.

You can also choose from a list of print options:

- **Print dark backgrounds as white**—This option simply saves printer ink. It prints dark backgrounds as white, reducing the amount of ink required to reproduce each slide.

- **Print each stage of builds**—When this option is selected, Keynote prints each stage of the build as a separate slide. Although this option can be effective in some cases, you should experiment to see how the print looks and whether the succession of slide builds is easy to read.

- **Include skipped slides**—If you have selected to skip any slides in your presentation, they are not printed by default. However, if you want to print them, just click this check box.

- **Add borders around slides**—This feature puts a border around each slide, making it look like a slide on the printed page. This option is selected by default.

- **Include slide numbers**—When this option is selected, the slide numbers are shown on the slides.

After you make selections, you can click the **Preview** button. Your Mac formats the print job as a PDF and opens Adobe Reader so you can preview everything and see how it will look. When you are happy, just close Acrobat Reader and click the Print button on the print dialog box. That's all there is to it!

Working with Presentation Hardware

Unless you are giving a presentation in a small conference room where the audience members can simply look at your Mac screen, you will probably be faced with some sort of presentation hardware connection. There is no need for this technological wonder to strike fear into your heart: Presentation hardware has become rather commonplace these days, and it is generally easy to use.

However, a word to the wise: Murphy's Law tells us that if something can go wrong, it certainly will. This sentiment is true with presentation hardware, also called AV equipment. You arrive at the conference room and the projector didn't show up, or even if it is there, it doesn't work and no one is available to help you. These happenings are common, so if you travel from place to place, making presentations, you should certainly be prepared for the unexpected.

The best advice I can give is an old public speaking piece of advice: You should be able to give a presentation without your Keynote slides. There, I said it (although you probably didn't want to hear it). In a technology age, we should certainly use technology, but we should not become so entrapped by it that we cannot function without it. Therefore, you should have a presentation polished enough that you can do it (and do it well) should you not be able to use your Keynote slides. This way, no matter what happens, you'll still be able to communicate your message to your audience.

With that said, the presentation hardware you are most likely to use is a projector of some kind. An AV projector connects to your computer and allows you to either display exactly the same thing as you see onscreen, or to present slides on the projector while you use the speaker notes onscreen. An AV projector is the standard kind of projector you see in conference rooms and larger auditoriums. If you are traveling from place to place, you might need an onsite technician to help you get everything connected because each projector brand works a bit differently.

> **tip**
>
> It is a good idea to print handout copies of a presentation so that you can give the handouts to your audience as a visual aid, in case you have equipment problems. Print these ahead of time and keep them on hand should you need them.

The three common projector types are LCD, DLP, and CRT.

LCD, or liquid crystal display, projectors have been used for a long time. They work well, but they tend not to display graphics too beautifully. Also, if you need to project a Keynote presentation onto a large screen, such as you might use with an audience of 100 people or more, LCD isn't your best choice because overall it does not provide the best resolution. Also, LCD projectors are not very bright, so you'll need a rather dark room for them to display well.

A *DLP*, or digital light processing, projector is a very good projector that uses digital processing and manages to keep the images in a presentation very sharp. DLP projectors are still rather new and are rather expensive as well. However, they do look great and are very bright, requiring less darkness in the room than an LCD projector.

CRT, or cathode ray tube, is a rather old technology, but it's still one that is commonly used with projectors. The best thing about CRT is that it tends to provide sharper images than LCD, and CRT projectors are commonly available for rent or purchase. Also, many conference rooms and auditoriums provide CRT projectors. Overall, a CRT projector provides a bright image, giving you more flexibility with room darkness.

You might not have much of a choice about which projector will be used, unless you have to provide your own. The key point is that you arrive at the meeting place in plenty of time to get any technical issues worked out. Have you ever seen a speaker who came into the room when the speech was supposed to start and then spent the next 10 minutes trying to get AV equipment to work? I thought so. Audience members do not appreciate this lack of organization and poor time management. So be sure to arrive early and give yourself plenty of time to get connected.

If you give a lot of presentations, you might consider purchasing your own projector, especially if you are having to foot the bill for renting one. If you use a projector a lot, you can recover the cost of it in a few months, and you'll get to use the same projector over and over without having to master a learning curve with each new projector you get. Of course, you'll have to haul it from place to place, so carefully weigh the advantages and disadvantages before parting with your hard-earned money.

AV projectors normally connect to your video ports or possibly even USB ports. If you are using an iBook or PowerBook, you might need the Apple VGA display adapter (which generally comes with your computer). The display adapter fits onto the Video Out port so that you can connect to the projector.

The Absolute Minimum

Keynote gives you the flexibility and the options you need when you make a presentation. Keep these points in mind:

- Use the Play button to play a slideshow, and keep in mind that you can use your keyboard arrow keys to move forward or backward during the show.

- You can export a Keynote presentation to a QuickTime movie format or to a PDF file. Click File, Export to start the process.

- You might need to use presentation hardware when you give a presentation. Keep in mind that most projectors work with a Mac without any problems, but allow yourself plenty of time to set up just in case something goes wrong.

IN THIS CHAPTER

- Create new themes for presentations
- Create new master slides to add a personal touch
- Use Keynote and Microsoft PowerPoint slideshows without any hassles

10

EXTENDING KEYNOTE

Keynote gives you everything you need right out of the gate. This keeps you from having to spend hours and hours creating custom content and graphics. However, what if you need to make some changes to the basics Keynote provides? What if you need to create a custom theme or custom master slides for a particular presentation? Or what if you need to export a presentation to a Microsoft PowerPoint format or even use a PowerPoint presentation from within Keynote? These are all common issues and challenges, and in this chapter, you'll see just how to manage them all.

Creating New Themes

Keynote's default themes work great, and they save you a lot of time and energy. However, there may come a time when you need to create a custom theme. Maybe you have a specific purpose in mind, or maybe you need a theme to adhere to some specific company colors, graphics, or other artwork.

In any case, you can create new themes in Keynote; you are not limited to the themes Keynote gives you. Creating new themes can be rather tedious, but the work isn't hard. Just be prepared to spend a little time working on it.

When you create a new theme in Keynote, you are actually editing and resaving an existing theme. This means that you change all of the theme's background colors, fonts, graphics, and anything else you want. That doesn't sound so bad, but the problem is that you have to change all the master slides as well, so you sort of have to do the process over and over until you make all the changes on all the master slides. As I said, it's not difficult, but it's tedious.

You might be forced to create a new theme, or you might be the creative type who really wants something different. In any case, you can create a theme just as you want it in Keynote, and the following sections show you how.

Selecting a Theme to Edit

To create a custom theme, the first thing you need to do is a select an existing theme. Keep in mind that in order to create a new theme, what you really do is edit an existing theme and save the new theme by another name.

In Keynote, you select **File**, **New**. The theme selection window appears, as you can see in Figure 10.1. You might want to select the White theme, just to keep things from being confusing, but before you do so, be sure to look at the existing themes. Are there any themes that resemble what you are after? If so, choosing one that already has your color scheme or layout style can make your editing process easier, as you'll have fewer elements to change.

When you have decided on a theme, select it and click **Choose Theme**. The theme appears in Keynote, with the default slide visible. Select **View**, **Show Master Slides**. The master slides appear in the Slide Organizer, as shown in Figure 10.2. You use the Show Master Slides feature because you have to edit all the master slides. At this point, you are ready to begin the editing process.

FIGURE 10.1

You choose a theme to edit.

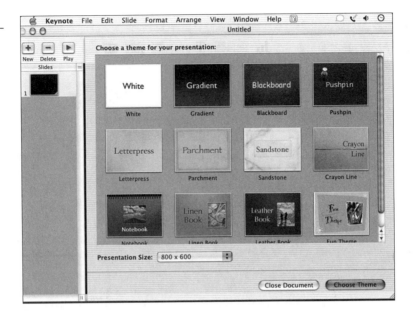

FIGURE 10.2

You choose View, Show Master Slides so that the master slides appear in the Slide Organizer.

Choosing a Background and Graphics

At this point, you need to select the Blank master slide in the Slide Organizer. Of course, you don't have to start with the blank slide, but because you want to format your background and any graphics first, it is easiest to start with the blank slide.

Now you are ready to work with the background. Follow these steps:

1. Click the **Inspector** button on the toolbar and then click the **Slide** button on the Inspector.

2. Under Background (see Figure 10.3), choose **Color Fill**, **Gradient Fill**, **Image Fill**, or **None** and then choose the options or import the desired image. This is the same background formatting trick you have used in other lessons. See Chapter 6, "Working with Backgrounds and Multimedia," for details.

tip

You can create custom backgrounds with your company logo (or anything else you might want) in any image-editing program. Just save your creation as a JPEG or TIFF file, and then you can import it to a slide as an image. This gives you a virtually unlimited number of background options.

FIGURE 10.3

You choose the desired background option.

3. When you have the background you want, place any additional graphics on the slide, such as your company logo or other objects.

4. When you are done and you are happy with the background, click every other master slide in the Slide Organizer and make the same changes to those slides. Unfortunately, there is no automated method for doing this, so you'll have spend a little time pointing and clicking to make all the changes.

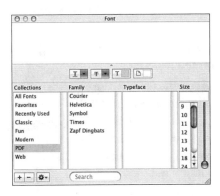

tip

When you create the first slide, be sure to write down the color values and other settings you apply to the first slide. Then you can simply repeat those settings on other master slides. Also, you might want to print your first master slide and mark it up with your setting values. Then you can use it as a guide as you work on the remainder of the master slides.

Editing Fonts and Styles

When you have the background of a theme changed as you like, your next task is to change the fonts and the styles used on those fonts, such as italic, bold, and so on. Follow these steps:

1. Select your first master slide (such as **Title & Subtitle**) in the Slide Navigator.

2. Select the first text block, such as the title text.

3. Click the **Fonts** button on the toolbar or select **Format**, **Font**. The Font dialog box appears.

4. In the Font dialog box, choose the font you want from the **Family** list, change the font size if needed, and then apply any desired styling, such as bold, italic, and so on, as shown Figure 10.4.

FIGURE 10.4

You choose the desired font and font characteristics.

5. If you want to make any changes to the text color, spacing, or bullets and numbering, open the Text Inspector and make those changes, as shown in Figure 10.5. See Chapter 2, "Working with Text," for details.

FIGURE 10.5

You can use the Text Inspector to make color, spacing, bullet, and numbering changes.

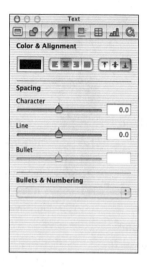

Repeat this process for all the other master slides, as necessary.

Customizing Chart Types

Chart formatting is determined by the theme you select, so you might consider changing the default chart formatting to something that works best for your custom theme. To do this, you create a master slide for your chart type. If you don't plan on using charts with your new theme, you can skip this section.

1. In the Slide Navigator, select the **Blank** master slide.

2. Choose **Edit**, **Copy** and then choose **Edit**, **Paste**. A copy of the blank slide is created.

3. With the copy of the blank master slide open, click the **Chart** button on the toolbar.

4. Click the **Inspector** button on the toolbar. Use the **Chart Inspector** to choose the kind of chart you want (column, pie, and so on). Using the **Text Inspector** and the **Color Inspector**, adjust the colors of the text and chart so that they look good with the background.

5. When you're done, set this chart as the default for your theme by selecting **Format**, **Define Defaults for Master Slides**, **Define Column Chart for Current Master**. If you want the chart style to apply to all your master slides, select **Format**, **Define Defaults for Master Slides**,

Note that you can make chart style, such as column chart, the default chart type. Just choose **Format, Define Defaults for Master Slides, Make Column Chart the Default Chart Type**.

Define Column Chart for All Masters, as shown in Figure 10.6. This ensures that any chart you create on any slide in the presentation will adhere to your new settings.

FIGURE 10.6

You can define a column chart for all your master slides.

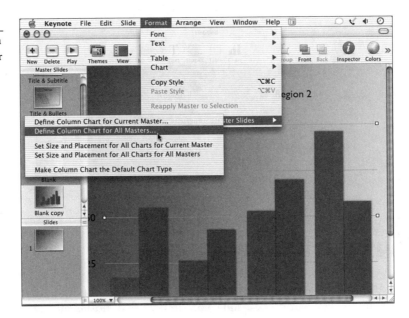

Saving a Custom Theme

When you have made all the desired changes and you have the custom theme you have always dreamed of (or at least wanted), all you have to do is save the custom theme. To do so, select **File**, **Save Theme**. Keynote saves your new theme with all your master slides, charts, text styles, and any other items you have defined on your master slide. When you select File, Save Theme, a dialog box appears, asking you to name the theme, and the theme is stored in Keynote's Themes folders by default. (You should leave it in that location.) Whenever you create a new presentation, your new theme will appear as an option in the themes list. As you can see in Figure 10.7, Curt's Theme is now an option I can choose. You can repeat this process over and over to create additional themes.

tip

If you want more themes but you want someone else to do the work, there are a number of Keynote themes you can download from the Web. See Appendix C, "Helpful Keynote Web Sites," for details.

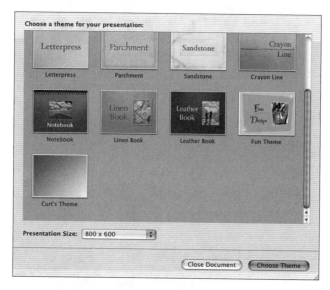

Creating New Master Slides

As you are well aware at this point, master slides give you a basic template to work with when you create slide content. Rather than having to create slides from scratch each time you want a new slide, you simply use a master slide and essentially fill in the gaps. However, what if there is a master slide that doesn't fit your needs? Or what if you want to create a custom master slide that you will use time and time again in a custom theme? In this case, you need to create a new master slide, which is basically a custom master slide that you can use any time you might need it.

Let's consider an example. Say that your company's marketing department requires that every presentation have the company logo on each Keynote slide. How can you make this happen without having to create a new custom slide each time you write a new presentation? You use a custom master slide. You simply create the master slide that contains your company logo and any other items that may be needed. Then you can simply select this master slide, regardless of what Keynote theme you use. The extra master slide with the required items greatly decreases your work because you have to create the master slide just one time.

You can create new master slides in much the same way that you create new themes. You simply copy an existing master slide, edit it, and then give it a new name. Then the new master slide will be associated with your theme, and you can use it any time you like.

To create a new master slide, just follow these steps:

1. Open a desired presentation and then select **View**, **Show Master Slides**.

2. Select the desired master slide in the Slide Navigator.

3. Choose **Edit**, **Copy** and then choose **Edit**, **Paste**. The pasted slide has the same name as the copied slide, with the word *copy* appended to it, as you can see in Figure 10.8. Double-click in the title of the copied slide and rename it as you wish.

4. Click the slide, and in the Slide Canvas, begin making any changes you want to the slide. Keep in mind that any changes you make become a part of the new master slide and will be available whenever you use the master slide.

After you make the changes, the new master slide appears in your master slide list. For example, as you can see in Figure 10.9, I have created a slide called Additional Bullets. I can now use this new master slide just as I would any other master slide.

FIGURE 10.9

A new slide now appears as a master slide.

Keynote and Microsoft PowerPoint

Consider this scenario: You use Keynote to create a presentation. You travel to a conference with your Mac where you will give your speech in a large conference room. The conference room is already outfitted with an AV projector and screen connected to a laptop computer. The laptop runs Microsoft Windows, and the place you are presenting will not let you use your Mac. You need to put your Keynote presentation on a disc and use it on the Windows computer for the presentation. Now what?

Or let's say that your company uses both Windows and Macintosh computers. You create a fantastic presentation with Keynote, but your salespeople want to use the presentation on Windows. Again, what do you do?

Like it or not, at some point you may need to use a Windows computer to give a presentation. Therefore, Keynote has the ability to work with Microsoft PowerPoint— without any additional work from you.

To use a presentation with Microsoft PowerPoint, all you have to do is export your Keynote presentation as a Microsoft PowerPoint document. You can then open and display your Keynote presentation from within Microsoft PowerPoint. You can also edit your presentation directly from within PowerPoint if you like.

To export a Keynote presentation to Microsoft PowerPoint, just follow these steps:

1. Open the Keynote presentation.

2. Select **File**, **Export**. An export dialog box appears.

3. In the export dialog box, click the **PowerPoint** radio button to select it and then click **Next** (see Figure 10.10).

FIGURE 10.10

You choose the PowerPoint option to export a Keynote presentation to PowerPoint.

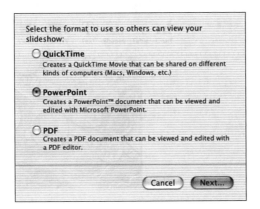

4. In the next dialog box that appears, give the presentation a name and choose where you want to save it. Then click **Export**. The presentation is exported and saved as a PowerPoint file.

You can now burn the presentation to a CD if you like and keep this converted Keynote presentation with you, just in case you need to play it within PowerPoint.

The subject of exporting a Keynote presentation to PowerPoint naturally begs the question "Can you import a PowerPoint document into Keynote?" Yes! Usually you can do this with no problems. Just select **File**, **Open**, select the PowerPoint presentation you want to import, and click **Open**. Keynote imports the PowerPoint presentation, typically without any problems. After you import the PowerPoint file, you can then edit it in Keynote and save it as a Keynote presentation. You can then export it back to PowerPoint if you like.

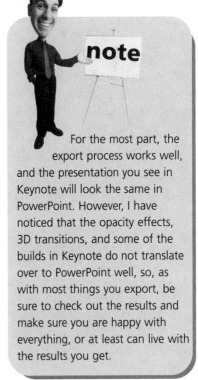

note

For the most part, the export process works well, and the presentation you see in Keynote will look the same in PowerPoint. However, I have noticed that the opacity effects, 3D transitions, and some of the builds in Keynote do not translate over to PowerPoint well, so, as with most things you export, be sure to check out the results and make sure you are happy with everything, or at least can live with the results you get.

THE ABSOLUTE MINIMUM

Keynote allows you to do great things! Keep these points in mind:

- You can edit existing Keynote themes and save them as new Keynote themes. Simply edit the master slides and select File, Save Theme to save the new theme you have created.

- You can edit and create new master slides. Simply copy an existing master slide and change it as you wish; then rename it. The new master slide will then be available for your use.

- Keynote works well with Microsoft PowerPoint. You use File, Export to export a presentation to the PowerPoint format. Also, you can directly import a PowerPoint presentation to Keynote by selecting File, Open and selecting the PowerPoint presentation.

A

INSTALLING KEYNOTE

The good news (and it's all good news) is that the simplest thing you'll probably do with Keynote is install it. In fact, as with most Mac applications, installation of Keynote is so easy that you'll need only a few mouse clicks to get the job done. If you feel a little trepidation about installing Keynote on your Mac, don't worry: This appendix is here to make sure your Mac is up to the task and guide you through the installation process, so read on!

Making Sure Your Mac Is Ready for Keynote

Like all software in the world today, Keynote has some restrictions and requirements that you need to know about. You need to pay attention to these restrictions and requirements if you want to install Keynote at all or at least watch it work without bringing your Mac to a snail's crawl. Here's what you need:

- Power Macintosh G3 or G4, eMac, or a 500MHz or faster iMac or iBook (PowerPC G4 recommended). I'm using Keynote on an 800MHz PowerPC G4 iMac, and it works great. If your Mac doesn't meet these requirements, you might still be able to install Keynote, but it might run terribly slowly.

- Mac OS X v10.2 or later. If you're not using Mac OS X v10.2 or later, consider upgrading your system to the latest Mac OS. Visit www.apple.com/macosx to learn more.

- 128MB of RAM minimum, with 512MB recommended. I'm using 256MB, and all works fine.

- 8MB of video memory, with 32MB recommended.

- 1GB of available disk space.

How can you make sure your system meets all of these requirements? There are two quick ways. First, click the **Apple** icon in the upper-left corner of your Mac screen and then click **About This Mac**. As you can see in Figure A.1, you can quickly see your Mac OS version, memory, and processor speed.

FIGURE A.1

You can check the About This Mac dialog box to see if your system meets the demands of Keynote.

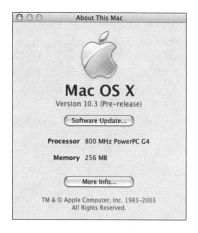

To make sure you have enough free disk space (at least 1GB), Control+click **Macintosh HD** on the desktop and click **Get Info**. The Macintosh HD Info dialog box appears, as shown in Figure A.2. It tells you how much of your disk you have used and how much is available. If you don't have quite enough disk space available, you might need to uninstall some applications you no longer need or move some files to another location in order to free up some needed disk space.

FIGURE A.2

You can check the Macintosh HD Info dialog box to make sure you have enough free disk space to install Keynote.

Installing Keynote

When you are sure your Mac is ready to handle the demands of Keynote, you are ready to install the software. Installation is quick and painless; just follow these steps:

1. Insert the Keynote installation CD-ROM into your Mac's CD-ROM drive.

2. The Keynote 1.0 CD window appears, showing you what is contained on the CD-ROM (see Figure A.3).

FIGURE A.3

The Keynote 1.0 folder shows what is on the CD-ROM.

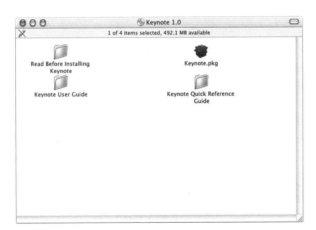

3. Double-click the **Keynote.pkg** icon to start the installation.

4. Type your administrator password in the dialog box that appears and click **OK**. Note that you must be logged on with an administrator account in order to install new software.

5. When the Keynote installer screen appears, read the introduction to Keynote and click the **Continue** button. The Read Me file appears, telling you about the system requirements for installing Keynote.

6. You can read the Read Me file if you like. Click **Continue** when you are ready to proceed.

7. When the License agreement appears, read it and then click **Continue**. In the dialog sheet that appears, click the **Agree** button. You must agree to the software license before installation will continue.

8. In the Select a Destination window, shown in Figure A.4, select your Macintosh HD for the installation. You must install Keynote on the primary computer's drive, so do not select an alternate location (such as a secondary disk drive), if one is available.

FIGURE A.4

You can Choose Macintosh HD for the installation and click Continue.

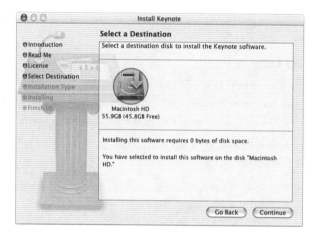

9. Click **Install** to start the installation. Keynote is installed on your Mac. The installation process may take several minutes.

10. Click **Close** when you are prompted.

That's all there is to it!

THE ABSOLUTE MINIMUM

Installing Keynote is a snap. Just remember these tips:

■ Make sure your Mac can handle the demands of Keynote. You need a Power Macintosh G3 or G4 processor, Mac OS X 10.2 or later, at least 128MB of RAM, at least 8MB of video memory, and 1GB of available disk space.

■ To install Keynote, insert the installation CD-ROM and then double-click the **Keynote.pkg** icon. Follow the simple setup instructions that appear.

KEYNOTE KEYBOARD SHORTCUTS

If you want to make Keynote work a bit faster for you, you should become familiar with the keyboard shortcuts listed in Table B.1. They can save you some mouse movements and speed up your work at the same time.

TABLE B.1   Keyboard Shortcuts

Shortcut	Description
Working with the Slide Canvas	
Tab	Moves from object to object on the Slide Canvas.
Shift+Tab	Goes backward from object to object on the Slide Canvas.
Arrow keys	Moves an object by one pixel at a time.
Shift+arrow keys	Moves an object by 10 pixels at a time
Shift+click or ⌘+click	Adds or removes the selected object to a previously selected object.
Shift+drag or ⌘+drag	Adds or removes the selected range to a previously selected object.
Shift+drag	Allows you to drag and control a selected item.
Option+drag	Duplicates an object, such as in a table or another slide element.
⌘+drag	Temporarily turns off the alignment guides on the Slide Canvas.
⌘+drag handle	Rotates the selected object.
⌘+Shift+drag handle	Rotates the selected object by 45°.
Shift+drag handle	Maintains an object's proportion when you're resizing it.
Option+drag handle	Resizes an object from the center out.
Option+Shift+drag handle	Maintains the proportion from the object's center position when you're resizing the object.
Page Down	Jumps to the next slide in the Slide Organizer.
Page Up	Jumps to the previous slide in the Slide Organizer.
Home	Jumps to the first slide in the presentation.
End	Jumps to the last slide in the presentation.
Control+click	Opens the contextual menus.
⌘+C	Copies the selected text or object on the slide.
⌘+V	Pastes the copied text or object on the slide.
⌘+X	Cuts the selected text or object from the slide to the Clipboard so that the object can be pasted elsewhere.
Working with Text	
Shift+right arrow	Extends the selection one character to the right.
Shift+left arrow	Adds one character to the left of a selection.
Option+right arrow	Moves to the end of the current word in which the cursor is placed.

TABLE B.1   (continued)

Shortcut	Description
Option+left arrow	Moves to the beginning of the current word in which the cursor is placed.
Shift+Option+right arrow	Adds what is selected to the end of the current word.
Shift+Option+left arrow	Adds what is selected to the beginning of the current word.
⌘+right arrow	Moves the cursor to the end of the line.
⌘+left arrow	Moves the cursor to the beginning of the line.
Shift+⌘+right arrow	Adds the selection to the end of the line.
Shift+⌘+left arrow	Adds the selection to the beginning of the line.
Up arrow	Jumps to the line above the current location.
Down arrow	Jumps to the line below the current location.
Shift+up arrow	Adds the selection to the line above it.
Shift+down arrow	Adds the selection to the line below it.
Option+up arrow	Moves to the beginning of the paragraph in which the cursor is placed.
Option+down arrow	Moves to the end of the paragraph in which the cursor is placed.
Shift+Option+up arrow	Moves the selection to the beginning of the paragraph.
Shift+Option+down arrow	Adds the selection to the end of the paragraph.
⌘+up arrow	Moves the cursor to the beginning of the text.
⌘+down arrow	Moves the cursor to the end of the selected text.
Shift+⌘+up arrow	Adds the selection to the beginning of the current text.
Shift+⌘+down arrow	Adds the selection to the end of the current text.
Delete	Deletes the previous character or the selection.
Option+Delete	Deletes the part of the word to the left of the cursor.
Page Up or Home	Scrolls to the top of the Slide Canvas.
Page Down or End	Scrolls to the bottom of the Slide Canvas.
⌘+Return	Selects the text box and stops editing the current text.
Playing a Slideshow	
Space or click or right arrow or down arrow or Page Down	Plays the next slide.
Left arrow or up arrow or Page Up	Plays the previous slide.
Esc or Q or ⌘+. (period)	Ends the slideshow.

TABLE B.1   (continued)

Shortcut	Description
B	Turns the screen to black. This is an effective way to pause a presentation so that audience members do not continue looking at the presentation content.
Home	Shows the first presentation slide.
End	Shows the last presentation slide.

Using the Slide Organizer

Return	Creates a new slide at the same Slide Organizer location as the previously selected slide.
Tab	Indents a slide in the Slide Organizer to the right.
Shift+Tab	Moves all selected indented slides in the Slide Organizer to the left.
Shift+click	Adds the current selection to the selected slide.
Shift+drag	Adds the selected range of slides to the previously selected slides.
⌘+click or Shift+click	Adds or removes the currently selected slide to the previously selected slides.
⌘+drag	Adds or removes the selected range to the previously selected slides.
Option+drag	Makes a copy of a slide.
Down arrow	Moves the selection to the next slide.
Shift+down arrow	Adds the next slide to the current selection.
⌘+down arrow	Selects the last slide in the Slide Organizer.
Shift+⌘+down arrow	Adds the current selection to the last slide.
Up arrow	Selects the previous slide in the Slide Organizer.
Shift+up arrow	Adds the current selection to the previous slide.
⌘+up arrow	Selects the first slide in the Slide Organizer.
Shift+⌘+up arrow	Adds the first slide to the current selection.
Delete	Deletes the selected slides.
Home	Scrolls to the first slide without changing the current selection.
End	Scrolls to the last slide without changing the current selection.
Page Down	Scrolls down one page of slides without changing the selection.
Page Up	Scrolls up one page of slides without changing the selection.

TABLE B.1   (continued)

Shortcut	Description
Working with Chart Data	
Return	Finishes a cell entry and moves the selection down one cell.
Shift+Return	Finishes a cell entry and moves the selection up one cell.
Tab	Finishes a cell entry and moves the selection to the right one cell.
Shift+Tab	Finishes a cell entry and moves the selection to the left one cell.
Home	Moves to the beginning of the current row.
End	Moves to the last nonblank cell to the right of the insertion point in the current row.
Moving Within Tables	
⌘+A	Selects all table cells, borders, or cell content, based on the initial selection.
⌘+C	Copies the contents of the selected cells or the whole table, depending on what is selected.
⌘+X	Deletes the contents of the selected cells or the whole table, depending on what is selected.
⌘+V	Pastes the last selection that was copied at the current insertion point.
Delete	Deletes whatever is selected.
Shift+drag table	Keeps the table in proportion and forces it to snap to the guides when you're moving it.
Option+Shift+drag table	Duplicates the table during a move.
Drag selected cell to another cell	Swaps the contents of the selected cell with the contents of the destination cell.
Option+drag selected cell to another cell	Copies the contents of the selected cell into the destination cell.
Shift+click ⌘+click selected or unselected cell	Adds selection from the selected cell to the destination cell. Adds or removes the selected cell to or from the current location.
⌘+Return; ⌘+click cell (in) text edit mode	Selects the cell and stops the editing of text.
Click+drag cell (in text edit mode)	Selects the text of a cell and then selects multiple cells while you drag the mouse.

TABLE B.1   (continued)

Shortcut	Description
Click border of selected table	Selects an entire row or column border.
Click+drag selected border or border segment of selected cell	Moves the selected row or column border to a different position.
Shift+arrow keys	Moves the selected table 10 pixels in the Slide Canvas. The direction of the move is determined by the arrow key used.
Shift+arrow keys (in cell selection mode)	Adds to the cell selection by one cell.
Shift+Tab	Selects text in the previous cell from the previous cursor location.
Control+Tab (in text edit mode)	Inserts a tab at the cursor insertion point.
⌘+Return (in cell selection mode)	Selects the table and stops editing of the current cell.

C

HELPFUL KEYNOTE WEB SITES

Keynote is such an easy and effective application that you are not likely to experience any major problems, and for those features you do have trouble using, you have this book to help you along. However, in case you have problems, the following are some places on the Internet you might like to try:

- **www.info.apple.com/usen/keynote**—This is the official Keynote support page, and it can be a great help. A number of known issues and problems, along with their solutions, are posted here, so if you are having problems, you should certainly check out this page.

- **www.apple.com/keynote**—Of course, a great place to start is Apple's Keynote site. You might not solve any problems here, but this site can alert you to updates and known issues. Also, you can check this site for update downloads that you might need.

- **http://discussions.info.apple.com**—This is a great place to find out what other people are saying about Keynote. You can ask a question of other Keynote enthusiasts, and you might find that your question has already been asked and answered on the discussion board.

- **www.keynotepro.com**—This is a good site that provides some great tips and tricks. This site also offers additional themes you can purchase.

- **www.keynoteuser.com**—This site has great resources, including themes, tips, tutorials, and even a good troubleshooting page. There is a lot of information here about all things Keynote, and you should certainly check it out—even if you are not having problems!

- **www.keynotegallery.com**—This site provides additional themes for sale at good prices (many of them under $10). You are sure to find some themes here that will liven up and coordinate with your presentation content.

- **www.keynotethemepark.com**—This site provides additional themes for purchase.

- **www.keynotehq.com**—This site provides Keynote themes, discussions, tips, tricks, and much more. Overall, it's a very helpful and fun site to visit.

- **www.mykeynotethemes.com**—This site provides additional Keynote themes, and you'll also find some good tutorials and other information here.

- **www.macworld.com**—Of course, this is a great site for all things Macintosh. You can search for articles and tutorials on this site.

Index

A

About This Mac command (Apple menu), 200

accessing master slides, 148-150

Add Column button, 77

Add Row button, 77

Add to Favorites option (Font dialog box), 37

Adobe Web site, 181

AIFF files, 127

aligning
graphics, 106-108
text, 40-41, 53-54

alignment guides
changing appearance of, 110
creating, 109
positioning graphics with, 106-108

All at Once option (chart/table builds), 165-166

alpha channels, 104

Apple menu commands
About This Mac, 200
System Preferences, 176

Apple Web site, 209-210

area charts, 72

audio
adding to slides, 128-129
AIFF files, 127
deleting from slides, 129
importing, 127-128
iTunes, 128-129
MP3 files, 127
repeat options, 129-131
volume, 129-131

AV projectors, 186

Axes & Borders option (axis markings), 82

axis markings
Axes & Borders, 82
Labels, Ticks, & Grids, 83
Number Format, 84
Value Axis Format, 84

B

Background First option (chart builds), 166

backgrounds
changing by combining themes, 120-122
changing with Slide Inspector, 118-120
custom themes, 190-192
table backgrounds, 61-62

bar charts, 70

Bar Format option (Chart Inspector), 85

Blank master slide, 146

books, *Special Edition Using Mac OS X, v10.3 Panther,* **131**

borders, 59-61

Build Inspector, 9, 161-163
chart builds, 165-167
image builds, 168
multiple-build slides, 168-171
table builds, 164-165
text builds, 163-164

builds, 6
advantages of, 160-161
Build Inspector, 161-163
chart builds, 165-167
creating, 24
defined, 23-24, 160
image builds, 168
multiple-build slides, 168-171
table builds, 164-165
text builds, 163-164

bulleted lists, 42-43

Bullets master slide, 146

buttons
Add Column, 77
Add Row, 77
Chart, 68
Edit Data, 73

Group, 110
Inspector, 24, 53
Masters, 13, 145
Merge Cells, 57
Metric, 104
New, 34, 49
Play, 22
Shapes, 18, 96
Split Columns, 57
Split Rows, 57
Text, 35
Ungroup, 110
View, 20

By Cell Content option (table builds), 165

By Cell option (table builds), 165

By Column Content option (table builds), 165

By Column option (table builds), 165

By Element in a Series option (chart builds), 166

By Element in a Set option (chart builds), 166

By Row Content option (table builds), 165

By Row option (table builds), 165

By Series option (chart builds), 166

By Set option (chart builds), 166

C

cathode ray tube (CRT), 185

CD-ROMs, installing Keynote from, 201-202

cells
backgrounds, 61-62
borders, 59-61

changing
alignment guide appearance, 110
backgrounds
combined themes, 120-122
Slide Inspector, 118-120
chart colors, 80
chart fonts, 81
fonts, 36
slide order, 138-140
text color, 39-40
transitions, 159

Characters option (Font dialog box), 38

chart builds, 165-167

Chart button, 68

Chart Data Editor, 15-16, 73-77

Chart Inspector, 9, 77-78, 192
axis markings, 82-84
data series formatting options, 84-85
Plot Row vs. Column option, 78
Show Legend option, 78

charts
adding to slides, 15-16
area charts, 72
axis markings
Axes & Borders, 82
Labels, Ticks, & Grids, 83
Number Format, 84
Value Axis Format, 84
bar charts, 70
chart builds, 165-167
Chart Data Editor, 15-16, 73-77
Chart Inspector, 77-78
axis markings, 82-84
data series formatting options, 84-85
Plot Row vs. Column option, 78
Show Legend option, 78
choosing chart style, 69-70
colors, 80
column charts, 70
creating, 67-68
custom themes, 192-193
data points, 74
data series
defined, 74
formatting, 84-85
data sets, 74
defined, 65
designing, 71
fonts, 81
keyboard shortcuts, 207
labels, 16
legends, 79-80
line charts, 71
pie charts, 73, 86-87
stacked area charts, 73
stacked bar charts, 71
stacked column charts, 70
when to use, 66-67

checking spelling, 152

Choose a Theme dialog box, 11

choosing
chart styles, 69-70
fonts, 28-30, 36-38
master slides, 145
number of columns/rows, 56
presentation size, 11
themes, 11-12
transitions, 158-159
views, 20

Color Inspector, 192

Color option (Font dialog box), 38

Color Palettes, 94

Color Sliders, 93

Color Wheel, 93

colors, 92
    charts, 80
    Color Inspector, 192
    Color Palettes, 94
    Color Sliders, 93
    Color Wheel, 93
    filling shapes with color,
       97-98
       color fill, 98
       gradient fill, 99
       image fill, 100
    Image Palettes, 95
    text, 39-40

Colors dialog box, 39-40, 92
    Color Palettes, 94
    Color Sliders, 93
    Color Wheel, 93
    Crayons, 95
    Image Palettes, 95

column charts, 70

columns, 56-57

combining
    images and shapes, 111-113
    themes, 120-122

commands
    Apple menu
       About This Mac, 200
       System Preferences, 176
    Define Defaults for Master
       Slides menu
       Define Column Chart for
         All Masters, 193
       Define Column Chart for
         Current Master, 192
       Make Column Chart the
         Default Chart Type, 192

Edit menu
    Copy, 55, 105, 192
    Find, 153
    Paste, 55, 106, 192
    Place, 96
    Spelling, 152
    Undo, 59, 103
    Undo Delete, 140
File menu
    Export, 178, 197
    Image Library, 124
    New, 11, 188
    Open, 197
    Open Image Library, 105
    Open Samples, 7
    Print Outline, 182
    Print Slides, 182
    Save As, 23
    Save Theme, 193
Fill menu
    Gradient Fill, 99
    Image Fill, 100
Font menu, Show Fonts, 36,
    52
Format menu
    Define Defaults for Master
       Slides, 192
    Font, 36, 52, 191
    Reapply Master to
       Selection, 45
Keynote menu, Preferences,
    110, 175
Place menu, Table, 49
Shadow menu, Individual, 87
Slide menu
    Don't Skip Slide, 144
    New Slide, 14
    Skip Slide, 144
View menu
    Outline, 20, 137
    Play Slideshow, 22
    Show Inspector, 53
    Show Master Slides, 195
    Show Notes, 9, 150

    Show Rulers, 45, 107-109
    Show Toolbar, 13
    Slide Only, 137

Copy command (Edit menu), 55, 105, 192

Crayons, 95

CRT (cathode ray tube), 185

Cube transitions, 158

custom themes
    backgrounds, 190-191
    chart types, 192-193
    fonts, 191-192
    graphics, 190-191
    saving, 193
    selecting theme to edit, 188
    styles, 191-192

D

Data Point Label option (Chart Inspector), 85

data points, 74

data series
    defined, 74
    formatting, 84-85

data sets, 74

Define Column Chart for All Masters command (Define Defaults for Master Slides menu), 193

Define Column Chart for Current Master command (Define Defaults for Master Slides menu), 192

Define Defaults for Master Slides command (Format menu), 192

Define Defaults for Master Slides menu commands
  Define Column Chart for All Masters, 193
  Define Column Chart for Current Master, 192
  Make Column Chart the Default Chart Type, 192

deleting text boxes, 34

design
  charts, 71
    axis markings, 82-84
    colors, 80
    data series, 84-85
    fonts, 81
    legends, 79-80
  text
    alignment, 40-41
    bulleted lists, 42-43
    color, 39-40
    fonts, 28-30, 36-38
    importing, 45
    jokes/puns, 33
    length of, 30
    main ideas, 31-32
    numbered lists, 42-43
    overcrowding, 33
    proofreading, 32
    readability, 28-30
    simplicity, 31
    spacing, 40-41
    tabs, 45

dialog boxes
  Choose a Theme, 11
  Colors, 39-40, 92
    Color Palettes, 94
    Color Sliders, 93
    Color Wheel, 93
    Crayons, 95
    Image Palettes, 95

Find, 153
Font, 36-38, 52, 81, 191
Macintosh HD Info, 200
Preferences, 175-176
Print, 182-184
Save As, 23
System Preferences, 176

digital light processing (DLP), 185

Dissolve transitions, 158

DLP (digital light processing), 185

Don't Skip Slide command (Slide menu), 144

dragging text, 55

drives, checking free disk space on, 200

Drop transitions, 158

E

Edit Data button, 73

Edit menu commands
  Copy, 55, 105, 192
  Find, 153
  Paste, 55, 106, 192
  Place, 96
  Spelling, 152
  Undo, 59, 103
  Undo Delete, 140

Edit Sizes option (Font dialog box), 38

editors, Chart Data Editor, 15-16, 73-77

Export command (File menu), 178, 197

exporting
  to PDF, 181-182
  presentations to PowerPoint, 196-197
  to QuickTime, 177-181

F

Fade Through Black transitions, 158

File menu commands
  Export, 178, 197
  Image Library, 124
  New, 11, 188
  Open, 197
  Open Image Library, 105
  Open Samples, 7
  Print Outline, 182
  Print Slides, 182
  Save As, 23
  Save Theme, 193

files
  audio files
    adding to slides, 128-129
    AIFF files, 127
    deleting from slides, 129
    importing, 127-128
    iTunes, 128-129
    MP3 files, 127
    repeat options, 129-131
    volume, 129, 131
  PDF files, exporting presentations to, 181-182
  Presentation Tips.key, 7

Fill menu commands
  Gradient Fill, 99
  Image Fill, 100

filling shapes with color, 97-98
  color fill, 98
  gradient fill, 99
  image fill, 100

Find command (Edit menu), 153

Find dialog box, 153

Flip transitions, 158

Font command (Format menu), 36, 52, 191

Font dialog box, 36-38, 52, 81, 191

Font menu commands, Show Fonts, 36, 52

fonts
changing, 36
charts, 81
choosing, 28-30, 36-38
Font dialog box, 36-38, 52

Format menu commands
Define Defaults for Master Slides, 192
Font, 36, 52, 191
Reapply Master to Selection, 45

formatting
charts
axis markings, 82-84
colors, 80
data series, 84-85
fonts, 81
legends, 79-80
numbers, 84
text, 51-53

free disk space, checking, 200

G

gradient fill, 99

Gradient Fill command (Fill menu), 99

Graphic Inspector, 9
fill options, 97
Color Fill, 98
Gradient Fill, 99
Image Fill, 100
shadows, 101-102
stroke options, 101

graphics, 89
adding to slides, 17-19
alignment guides
changing appearance of, 110
creating, 109
positioning graphics with, 106-108
bullets, 43
colors, 92
Color Palettes, 94
Color Sliders, 93
Color Wheel, 93
Crayons, 95
Image Palettes, 95
combining images and shapes, 111-113
combining with text, 114
custom themes, 190-191
explaining text with, 90
filling with color, 97-98
color fill, 98
gradient fill, 99
image fill, 100
grouping/ungrouping, 110
image builds, 168
image fill, 100
Image Library, 105-106
opacity, 19
photos
alpha channels, 104
importing, 103
resizing, 103-104
when to use, 92
rotating, 97
shadows, 101-102
shapes
adding to slides, 96-97
when to use, 91
stroke options, 101
tables, 62-63
when to use, 90-92

grids, 83

Group button, 110

grouping
objects, 110
slides, 21-22, 140-142

guides (alignment)
changing appearance of, 110
creating, 109
positioning graphics with, 106-108

H-I

handouts, 183

hard drives, checking free disk space on, 200

hardware, 184-186, 200

image builds, 168

image fill, 100

Image Fill command (Fill menu), 100

Image Library, 105-106, 124

Image Palettes, 95

images. *See* **graphics**

importing
audio, 127-128
photos, 103
presentations, 12
text, 45

Individual command (Shadow menu), 87

Inspector button, 24, 53

inspectors, 9-10
  Build Inspector, 9, 161-163
    chart builds, 165-167
    image builds, 168
    multiple-build slides,
      168-171
    table builds, 164-165
    text builds, 163-164
  Chart Inspector, 9, 77-78,
    192
    axis markings, 82-84
    data series formatting
      options, 84-85
    Plot Row vs. Column
      option, 78
    Show Legend option, 78
  Color Inspector, 192
  Graphic Inspector, 9
    fill options, 97-100
    shadows, 101-102
    stroke options, 101
  Metric Inspector, 9, 104
  QuickTime Inspector, 9
  Slide Inspector, 9, 156, 159
  Table Inspector, 9, 57
    cell backgrounds, 61-62
    cell borders, 59-61
    columns, 56-57
    images, 62
    rows, 56-57
  Text Inspector, 9, 39, 192
    text alignment, 40-41
    text color, 39-40
    text spacing, 40-41
installing Keynote, 199
  hardware/software require-
    ments, 200
  step-by-step instructions,
    201-202
iTunes, 128-129

J-K

jokes, 33

keyboard shortcuts, 203
  charts, 207
  slide canvas, 204
  Slide Organizer, 206
  slideshows, 205-206
  tables, 207-208
  text, 204-205
Keynote installation, 199
  hardware/software require-
    ments, 200
  step-by-step instructions,
    201-202
Keynote menu commands,
  Preferences, 110, 175
Keynote Web site, 209
KeynoteGallery.com Web
  site, 210
KeynoteHQ.com Web site,
  210
KeynotePro.com Web site,
  210
KeynoteThemePark.com Web
  site, 210
KeynoteUser.com Web site,
  210

L

labels (charts), 16, 83
Labels, Ticks, & Grids option
  (axis markings), 83
LCD (liquid crystal display),
  185
left aligning text, 40-41
legends, 79-80

length of text, 30
Library (Image Library),
  105-106, 124
line art. *See* **shapes**
line charts, 71
liquid crystal display (LCD),
  185
lists, 42-43
looping audio, 130

M

Macintosh HD Info dialog
  box, 200
MacWorld Web site, 210
main ideas, highlighting with
  text, 31-32
Make Column Chart the
  Default Chart Type com-
  mand (Define Defaults for
  Master Slides menu), 192
Manage Fonts option (Font
  dialog box), 38
master slides, 144
  accessing, 148-150
  Blank, 146
  Bullets, 146
  choosing, 145
  creating, 194-195
  defined, 11-12
  Title & Bullets, 146
  Title & Subtitle, 146
  Title — Center, 147
  Title — Horizontal, 147
  Title — Top, 146
  Title — Vertical, 147
  Title and Bullets Left, 148
  Title and Bullets Right, 148
  Title, Bullets & Photo, 148
  when to use, 145

Masters button, 13, 145

Media Inspector, 130

memory requirements, 200

Merge Cells button, 57

merging columns/rows, 57

Metric button, 104

Metric Inspector, 9, 104

Microsoft PowerPoint, exporting presentations to, 196-197

Mosaic transitions, 158

Motion Dissolve transitions, 158

Move In transitions, 158

movies, 131-133
    QuickTime presentations, 177-181

moving
    chart legends, 79-80
    text, 55
    through tables, 50

MP3 files, 127

multiple-build slides, 168-171

MyKeynoteThemes.com Web site, 210

N

navigating tables, 50

Navigator view, 8, 136-137

New button, 34, 49

New command (File menu), 11, 188

New Slide (Slide menu), 14

None transition setting, 158

notes (speaker), 150

Number Format option (axis markings), 84

numbered lists, 42-43

numbers
    chart number formats, 84
    numbered lists, 42-43

O

objects. *See also* **graphics**
    grouping/ungrouping, 110
    opacity setting, 122-126
    rotating, 97

opacity, 19, 122-126

Open command (File menu), 197

Open Image Library command (File menu), 105

Open Samples command (File menu), 7

organizing slides
    grouping slides, 21-22
    rearranging slides, 21-22
    views, 20

orientation of transitions, 159

Outline command (View menu), 20, 137

Outline view, 8, 137

outlines, 182

overcrowded text, 33

P

palettes
    Color Palettes, 94
    Image Palettes, 95

Paste command (Edit menu), 55, 106, 192

PDF files, exporting presentations to, 181-182

photos
    alpha channels, 104
    Image Library, 105-106
    importing, 103
    resizing, 103-104
    when to use, 92

pictures. *See* **photos**

pie charts, 73, 86-87

Pivot transitions, 158

Place command (Edit menu), 96

Place menu commands, Table, 49

Play button, 22

playing slideshows, 22, 174

Plot Row vs. Column option (Chart Inspector), 78

PowerPoint, exporting presentations to, 196-197

preferences
    alignment guides, 110
    slideshow viewing preferences, 175-177

Preferences command (Keynote menu), 110, 175

Preferences dialog box, 175-176

Presentation Tips.key file, 7

presentations, 10. *See also*
graphics; slides
  exporting to PDF, 181-182
  exporting to PowerPoint,
    196-197
  exporting to QuickTime,
    177-181
  importing, 12
  presentation hardware,
    184-186
  printing, 182-184
  sample presentation, 7-8
  saving, 23
  size of, 11
  speaker notes, 150
  video, 131-133
    mirroring, 177
    QuickTime presentations,
    177-181
  views, 136-137

Print dialog box, 182-184

**Print Outline command (File
menu), 182**

**Print Slides command (File
menu), 182**

printing
  handouts, 183
  outlines, 182
  presentations, 182-184
  slides, 182-184

projectors, 185-186

proofreading text, 32

puns, 33

Push transitions, 158

Q-R

QuickTime Inspector, 9

**QuickTime presentations,
177-181**

**Reapply Master to Selection
command (Format menu),
45**

**rearranging slides, 21-22,
138-140**

**repeat options (audio),
129-131**

**Replace & Find feature,
152-153**

resizing photos, 103-104

Reveal transitions, 158

rotating objects, 97

rows, 56-57

S

sample presentation, 7-8

**Save As command (File
menu), 23**

Save As dialog box, 23

**Save Theme command (File
menu), 193**

saving
  custom themes, 193
  presentations, 23

Scale transitions, 158

selection handles, 34

**Shadow menu commands,
Individual, 87**

shadows, 101-102

shapes
  adding to slides, 96-97
  combining with images,
    111-113
  filling with color, 97-98
    color fill, 98
    gradient fill, 99
    image fill, 100
  rotating, 97
  shadows, 101-102
  stroke options, 101
  when to use, 91

Shapes button, 18, 96

**Show Fonts command (Font
menu), 36, 52**

**Show Inspector command
(View menu), 53**

**Show Legend option (Chart
Inspector), 78**

**Show Master Slides com-
mand (View menu), 195**

**Show Notes command (View
menu), 9, 150**

**Show Rulers command (View
menu), 45, 107-109**

**Show Toolbar (View menu),
13**

**Show/Hide Effects option
(Font dialog box), 38**

**Show/Hide Preview option
(Font dialog box), 37**

simplicity of text, 31

size of presentations, 11

sizing photos, 103-104

**Skip Slide command (Slide
menu), 144**

skipping slides, 143-144

Slide Canvas, 8

slide canvas, keyboard short-cuts, 204

Slide Inspector, 9
backgrounds, changing, 118-120
opening, 156
transition options, 156, 159

Slide menu commands
Don't Skip Slide, 144
New Slide, 14
Skip Slide, 144

Slide Only command (View menu), 137

Slide Only view, 137

Slide Organizer, 8
keyboard shortcuts, 206

slides. *See also* **presentations; slideshows**
adding, 13-14
audio
adding, 128-129
AIFF files, 127
deleting, 129
importing, 127-128
iTunes, 128-129
MP3 files, 127
repeat options, 129, 131
volume, 129, 131
backgrounds
changing by combining themes, 120-122
changing with Slide Inspector, 118-120
builds, 6
advantages of, 160-161
Build Inspector, 161-163
chart builds, 165-167
creating, 24
defined, 23-24, 160
image builds, 168

multiple-build slides, 168-171
table builds, 164-165
text builds, 163-164
charts
adding, 15-16
area charts, 72
axis markings, 82-84
bar charts, 70
Chart Data Editor, 15-16, 73-77
Chart Inspector, 77-78, 82-85
choosing chart style, 69-70
colors, 80
column charts, 70
creating, 67-68
data points, 74
data series, 74, 84-85
data sets, 74
defined, 65
designing, 71
fonts, 81
keyboard shortcuts, 207
labels, 16
legends, 79-80
line charts, 71
pie charts, 73, 86-87
stacked area charts, 73
stacked bar charts, 71
stacked column charts, 70
when to use, 66-67
graphics, 89
adding to slides, 17-19
alignment guides, 106-110
bullets, 43
colors, 92-95
combining images and shapes, 111-113
combining with text, 114
custom themes, 190-191

explaining text with, 90
filling with color, 97-100
grouping/ungrouping, 110
image builds, 168
image fill, 100
Image Library, 105-106
opacity, 19
photos, 92, 103-104
rotating, 97
shadows, 101-102
shapes, 91, 96-97
stroke options, 101
tables, 62-63
when to use, 90-92
grouping, 21-22, 140-142
master slides, 144
accessing, 148-150
Blank, 146
Bullets, 146
choosing, 145
creating, 194-195
defined, 11-12
Title & Bullets, 146
Title & Subtitle, 146
Title — Center, 147
Title — Horizontal, 147
Title — Top, 146
Title — Vertical, 147
Title and Bullets Left, 148
Title and Bullets Right, 148
Title, Bullets & Photo, 148
when to use, 145
objects
grouping/ungrouping, 110
opacity setting, 122-126
rotating, 97
organizing
grouping slides, 21-22
rearranging slides, 21-22
views, 20

How can we make this index more useful? Email us at indexes@quepublishing.com

printing, 182-184
rearranging, 21-22
reordering, 138, 140
Replace & Find feature,
  152-153
skipping, 143-144
slide canvas, 204
Slide Inspector, 156, 159
Slide Organizer, 206
speaker notes, 150
spell check, 151-152
tables, 14, 47-48
  cell backgrounds, 61-62
  cell borders, 59-61
  columns, 56-57
  creating, 49
  images, 62-63
  moving around in, 50
  rows, 56-57
  text alignment, 53-54
  text entry, 51-53
  text formatting, 51-53
  text tips and techniques,
    55
  when to use, 48-49
text
  adding, 12-13, 33-34
  alignment, 40-41
  bulleted lists, 42-43
  color, 39-40
  combining with graphics,
    114
  fonts, 28-30, 36-38
  importing, 45
  jokes/puns, 33
  keyboard shortcuts,
    204-205
  length of, 30
  main ideas, 31-32
  numbered lists, 42-43
  overcrowding, 33
  proofreading, 32
  readability, 28-30

  simplicity, 31
  spacing, 40-41
  tabs, 45
  text boxes, 34-35
  Text Inspector, 39-41
themes
  choosing, 11-12
  combining, 120-122
  custom themes, 188-193
  defined, 11
transitions
  changing, 159
  choosing, 158-159
  creating, 156
  Cube, 158
  defined, 6, 25, 156
  Dissolve, 158
  Drop, 158
  Fade Through Black, 158
  Flip, 158
  Mosaic, 158
  Motion Dissolve, 158
  Move In, 158
  None setting, 158
  orientation, 159
  Pivot, 158
  Push, 158
  Reveal, 158
  Scale, 158
  setting up, 156-157
  speed, 159
  Twirl, 158
  Wipe, 158
video, 131-133
  mirroring, 177
  QuickTime presentations,
    177-181
views, 20

slideshows. *See also* **presentations; slides**
keyboard shortcuts, 205-206
playing, 22, 174
viewing preferences, 175-177

software requirements, 200
sound. *See* **audio**
spacing text, 40-41
speaker notes, 150
*Special Edition Using Mac OS
  X, v10.3 Panther*, **131**
speed of transitions, 159
spell check, 151-152
**Spelling command (Edit
  menu), 152**
Split Columns button, 57
Split Rows button, 57
splitting columns/rows, 57
stacked area charts, 73
stacked bar charts, 71
stacked column charts, 70
stroke options, 101
**styles, custom themes,
  191-192**
**System Preferences command
  (Apple menu), 176**
**System Preferences dialog
  box, 176**
system requirements, 200

T

table builds, 164-165
**Table command (Place menu),
  49**
Table Inspector, 9
cell backgrounds, 61-62
cell borders, 59-61
columns, 56-57
images, 62-63
rows, 56-57

tables, 47-48
  adding to slides, 14
  cell backgrounds, 61-62
  cell borders, 59-61
  columns, 56-57
  creating, 49
  images, 62-63
  keyboard shortcuts, 207-208
  moving around in, 50
  rows, 56-57
  table builds, 164-165
  text alignment, 53-54
  text entry, 51-53
  text formatting, 51-53
  text tips and techniques, 55
  when to use, 48-49

tabs, 45

text
  adding to slides, 12-13,
    33-34
  alignment, 40-41
  bulleted lists, 42-43
  color, 39-40
  combining with graphics,
    114
  explaining text with, 90
  fonts
    changing, 36
    charts, 81
    choosing, 28-30, 36-38
    Font dialog box, 36-38
  importing, 45
  jokes/puns, 33
  keyboard shortcuts, 204-205
  length of, 30
  main ideas, 31-32
  numbered lists, 42-43
  overcrowding, 33
  proofreading, 32
  readability, 28-30
  simplicity, 31
  spacing, 40-41

table text
  aligning, 53-54
  dragging, 55
  entering, 51-53
  formatting, 51-53
  moving, 55
  tips and techniques, 55
  tabs, 45
  text boxes, 34-35
  text builds, 163-164
  Text Inspector, 9, 192
    text alignment, 40-41
    text color, 39-40
    text spacing, 40-41

text boxes, 34-35

text builds, 163-164

Text button, 35

Text Inspector, 9, 192
  text alignment, 40-41
  text color, 39-40
  text spacing, 40-41

themes
  choosing, 11-12
  combining, 120-122
  custom themes
    backgrounds, 190-191
    chart types, 192-193
    fonts, 191-192
    graphics, 190-191
    saving, 193
    *selecting theme to edit,
      188*
    styles, 191-192
  defined, 11

ticks, 83

**Title & Bullets master slide,
  146**

**Title & Subtitle master slide,
  146**

**Title — Center master slide,
  147**

**Title — Horizontal master
  slide, 147**

Title — Top master slide, 146

**Title — Vertical master slide,
  147**

**Title and Bullets Left master
  slide, 148**

**Title and Bullets Right master
  slide, 148**

**Title, Bullets & Photo master
  slide, 148**

toolbar, 9. *See also* **buttons**

transitions
  changing, 159
  choosing, 158-159
  creating, 156
  Cube, 158
  defined, 6, 25, 156
  Dissolve, 158
  Drop, 158
  Fade Through Black, 158
  Flip, 158
  Mosaic, 158
  Motion Dissolve, 158
  Move In, 158
  None setting, 158
  orientation, 159
  Pivot, 158
  Push, 158
  Reveal, 158
  Scale, 158
  setting up, 156-157
  speed, 159
  Twirl, 158
  Wipe, 158

Twirl transitions, 158

typefaces. *See* **fonts**

U-V

Undo command (Edit menu), 59, 103

Undo Delete command (Edit menu), 140

undoing mistakes, 140

Ungroup button, 110

ungrouping objects, 110

Value Axis Format option (axis markings), 84

video, 131-133
   mirroring, 177
   QuickTime presentations, 177-181

View button, 20

View menu commands
   Outline, 20, 137
   Play Slideshow, 22
   Show Inspector, 53
   Show Master Slides, 195
   Show Notes, 9, 150
   Show Rulers, 45, 107-109
   Show Toolbar, 13
   Slide Only, 137

viewing slideshows, 174-177

views, 8
   choosing, 20
   Navigator view, 136-137
   Outline view, 137
   Slide Only view, 137

volume, 129-131

W-Z

Web sites
   Adobe, 181
   Apple, 209-210
   KeynoteGallery.com, 210
   KeynoteHQ.com, 210
   KeynotePro.com, 210
   KeynoteThemePark.com, 210
   KeynoteUser.com, 210
   MacWorld, 210
   MyKeynoteThemes.com, 210

Wipe transitions, 158

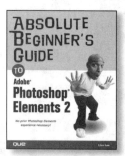